the NATURALLY
CLEAN HOME

150

Nontoxic Recipes for
Cleaning and Disinfecting
with ESSENTIAL OILS

Third Edition

KARYN SIEGEL-MAIER

Storey Publishing

The mission of Storey Publishing is to serve our customers by publishing practical information that encourages personal independence in harmony with the environment.

Edited by Hannah Fries
Art direction and book design by Alethea Morrison
Text production by Slavica A. Walzl
Indexed by Samantha Miller
Cover photography by © Bill Oxford/Getty Images (sponges);
© Floortje/iStock.com (lavender); © iprogressman/iStock.com
(hands with dropper and bottle); © Jiri Hera/stock.adobe.com (sage);
© LoveTheWind/iStock.com (bubbles and jar of oil); © Pranee
Tiangkate/iStock.com (rosemary); © vmenshov/stock.adobe.com
(orange)
Illustrations by © Kim Rosen
Text © 1999, 2008, 2021 by Karyn Siegel-Maier

Storey Publishing
210 MASS MoCA Way
North Adams, MA 01247
storey.com

Printed in the United States by Versa Press
10 9 8 7 6 5 4 3 2 1

Library of Congress Cataloging-in-Publication Data on file

CONTENTS

....

*This book is dedicated to you, the reader, whose commitment to
better living is my inspiration and reward for writing it.*

....

Acknowledgments

*Warm thanks to my family, friends, and online community members
for all the inspiration, feedback, and support over the years. Your
encouragement is the driving force that motivates me every day.*

*I'd also like to express my appreciation for the honor of being a
member of Storey's family of authors. In particular, special thanks
to Deborah Balmuth, Hannah Fries, and Paula Brisco for helping to
give new life to these pages to reach a new generation of readers.*

....

THE SCIENCE OF CLEAN

CLEANING WITH SOME FORM OF SOAP AND WATER has been around nearly as long as dirt. Early humans quickly realized that wading into a lake, river, or stream was an effective way to cool off and loosen the mud from their feet. Archaeological evidence suggests that the ancient Babylonians were the first to bring water, animal fat, and ash together to make soap sometime around 2200 BCE.

Since then, our soap and cleaning agents have evolved a great deal, but our desire to ever improve them eventually made them toxic to us and the planet. The goal of this book is to help you reduce your exposure to potentially hazardous chemicals, make more environmentally sustainable choices, and harness the power of nature to clean more safely and effectively with pure, simple ingredients, including essential oils.

Coming Clean about Soap

Water alone cannot clean surfaces because it has a property called surface tension. In other words, it can't reach the surface where the crud resides because it just beads up and stubbornly refuses to spread out. The trick to getting water to behave as we want it to on countertops and fabrics is to introduce a surfactant to reduce water tension. This is where soap comes in.

Soap is a surfactant that makes water molecules more slippery and better able to get down to the business of lifting dirt and grease. The earliest liquid soaps were made from olive and palm oils and saponins, chemical compounds found in certain plants (for example, soapwort) that foam when mixed with

water. For thousands of years, bar soap was made using animal fats until a supply shortage during World War I inspired German scientists to develop a synthetic surfactant, creating the first detergent. Since then, detergents have been "improved" with the addition of phosphate compounds and other chemicals. These chemicals are abundant in many types of household cleaners and even personal-care products like hand soap and shampoo. They have also found their way into the ecosystem, where they adversely impact marine life and inhibit the breakdown of other toxic substances in the environment.

These chemicals affect human health as well. For example, SDBS (sodium dodecylbenzene sulfonate) is a widely used surfactant that is absorbed through the skin and is known to be carcinogenic and damaging to the liver. The formulas in this book ask you to use castile soap, a vegetable-based soap made from olive, hemp, or coconut oil that is free of synthetic surfactants or detergents.

THE DANGERS OF BLEACH

Bleach, or sodium hypochlorite, is a combination of chlorine and sodium hydroxide (caustic soda) and is perhaps one of the most difficult of commercial cleaning products to relinquish. Technically speaking, household bleach is not considered corrosive or toxic, even if ingested. It is, however, classified as a skin and eye irritant. It can burn human tissue, internally or externally, especially in small children. In fact, the accidental swallowing of bleach is the most frequently received call at poison control centers involving children under the age of six. But young, tender hands and lips can also suffer serious burns.

If household bleach can do such damage, and is so predominantly a factor in the accidental poisoning of young children, why keep it around the house? There are many natural and nontoxic solutions for removing stains and keeping whites white. If you feel you must have access to a bottle of bleach, at least use one that is free of chlorine to reduce the risks. One of the best that I have used is made by Seventh Generation, whose products can often be found in health food stores and in some supermarkets. Treat this bleach as you would any other: Store it in a locked cabinet or out of reach of pets and children.

Getting Back to "Natural"

It's fair to say that "natural cleaning" isn't a new concept. If you're old enough to reminisce about Woodstock, then you're aware that the movement to stem the flow of toxins in our lives and in our environment has shifted from the outer fringe to the mainstream. By the mid-1990s, "green" products had hit the market in a big way. Unfortunately, a lack of regulation has led to "greenwashing," meaning that some companies are using misleading language to describe their products as "all-natural" when they actually are not.

No regulatory definitions exist for words like *all-natural* and *nontoxic,* making them meaningless on a product label unless a certification seal of a recognized, independent third party, such as the Environmental Protection Agency (EPA), backs up such claims. So, until these manufacturers clean up their act (and, to be fair, many are finally responding to consumer demand for safer products), we all need to be expert label readers and ingredient detectives. The ultimate solution? Make it yourself, and keep more green in your wallet!

A BOTANICAL BOOST

The most potent weapons against germs and grime in your natural cleaning products are essential oils. Combined with baking soda, vinegar, and other natural agents that reduce the surface tension of water, botanical essential oils increase the power of a homemade cleanser considerably. We'll get to how in a moment, but first, let's talk about what an essential oil is. Also known as a volatile oil because it has a fairly fast evaporation rate, an essential oil is a concentration of aromatic chemical compounds extracted from the root, leaf, wood, bark, fruit, flower, or seed of a plant, usually by steam distillation. The oil is called "essential" because it contains the essence of the fragrance profile of the plant from which it is obtained.

You may be new to using essential oils for cleaning your house, but I guarantee there are scores of them in your home at any given time. Essential oils are used to enhance flavor and extend the shelf life of many foods and beverages; they lend fragrance to perfumes; they are used in cosmetics to benefit skin and hair; and they are widely used in the pharmaceutical industry. You can't open a pantry door or medicine cabinet without coming face-to-face with a variety of essential oils.

FLOWER POWER

Here comes the "how" part. An essential oil may contain well over 300 compounds, but each belongs to one of two groups: hydrocarbons, which are largely terpenes (sesquiterpenes, diterpenes, and monoterpenes), and terpenoid compounds that contain oxygen in their chemical structure (alcohols, esters, aldehydes, ketones, phenols, and oxides). Collectively, these phytochemicals are responsible for the medicinal properties of many plants. They also serve as germ-fighting soldiers in the battle against not only dirt and grime but also bacteria and viruses.

For example, sesquiterpenes, such as carvacrol and linalool, are highly antiseptic and antimicrobial and are found in many common herbs.

A recent study published in the journal *Pathogens* showed that the essential oils of oregano, thyme, lemon, and lavender are effective against a number of common pathogens, including *Staphylococcus* strains and E. coli. A group of scientists from Wrocław University of Environmental and Life Sciences in Poland have identified a dozen essential oils with high antimicrobial activity, most notably lavender, thyme, peppermint, cajuput, cinnamon, eucalyptus, clove, sage, and tea tree. Citrus essential oils — lime, lemon, and sweet orange — are the workhorses of many kitchen and bath cleaners due to their content of limonene, a natural solvent and antibacterial agent found in the peel of these fruits. This list is by no means complete, but these are the essential oils most used in the formulas throughout this book.

Aren't Essential Oils Expensive?

Some are, yes. Sandalwood, bergamot, and patchouli oils, for example, may provide antimicrobial properties, but they are cost prohibitive for most of our cleaning purposes. Save those oils for your homemade perfumes, special skin-care formulas, and the like. Note, however, that you may want to consider adding a few drops of these highly aromatic oils to a product designed to fragrance your home, such as aroma sprays, linen sachets, herbal dream pillows, and potpourri. Some of the recipes in this book for herbal mists and potpourri blends contain ginger, vetiver, bergamot, and other fragrant essential oils. If you already have these oils among your herbal supplies, you're one step ahead. But feel free to experiment and to make substitutions when necessary.

Otherwise, the essential oils recommended in this book are quite economical. Consider for a moment that the purchase of a store-bought cleaner can average $3 or more, depending on the specific product and brand. In fact, the average American household spends nearly $200 annually for one-time-use laundry and cleaning products. Depending on the type and brand, a half ounce of the essential oils recommended in this book will average anywhere from $6 to $12, and each contains approximately 300 drops. Since each formula in this book uses anywhere from just a few drops up to 25 or 30, that little bottle will go a very long way indeed. As an added bonus, you won't be spending money on single-use packaging.

Quality and Purity

I personally make it a point to buy only certified organic essential oils, which adds to the price, but that's just me. In my home office, I have an apothecary cabinet that houses a large collection of jars filled with dried herbs, roots, barks, berries, and infused oils for making salves, along with a shelf of about 30 bottles of essential oils (in alphabetical order) and other liquid substances — rosemary extract, benzoin, vitamin E, glycerin, etc. I don't separate materials used for making medicines or cosmetics from those used for other herbal crafts, such as making natural cleaners. It's entirely up to you, but be prepared to pay a bit more for organic essential oils if you decide to follow this route.

Purity, on the other hand, does matter. Be sure to purchase oils from a reputable company, and consider those that embrace fair-trade practices that promote sustainable economies in the regions from which the oils are sourced. **The bottle should be labeled "100% pure essential oil."** (The label may also state that the oil is "therapeutic grade" or "clinical grade," meaning it is suitable for aromatherapy applications, although there is no regulatory definition for these terms.) If the bottle does *not* say it is 100 percent pure essential oil, you may be purchasing a fragrance oil. Such oils are fine for scenting candles, but they contain synthetic agents and are void of antimicrobial properties.

A WORD ABOUT SAFETY

Although the ingredients you will be using to make cleaning formulas are of organic origin, that doesn't mean they are without consequences if ingested.

Essential oils are highly concentrated forms of the volatile oils found in plants and should never be used internally. Just a few drops are equivalent to approximately 30 or 40 cups of herbal tea. Take special care with food-related oils; citrus oil, for example, could offer a temptation to a young child who may mistake a finished product as something delicious to eat or drink. Also, some essential oils, and other materials recommended in this book, can be irritating to the skin.

Please exercise the same caution with these herbal cleaning formulas as you would with any commercial cleaner, and keep them away from pets and children.

Getting Started

Now, you may be wondering what you need to get started making and using all-natural cleaning products. The following must-have items will create a large variety of cleaners for all sorts of different surfaces and jobs.

SUPPLIES AT A GLANCE

The basic supplies required for making your own cleaners are generally inexpensive and easy to find. To make the widest array of products for the home, the following are the items to have on hand.

Baking soda. Otherwise known as bicarbonate of soda, you can find this ingredient very inexpensively at any supermarket or grocery store, usually in the baking supplies aisle.

Beeswax. This solid substance, usually in chunk or brick form, is available at art and craft stores, candle supply shops, and sometimes from local beekeepers.

Carnauba wax. The hardest natural wax known, made from a Brazilian palm tree, this item is sold by furniture stores and mail-order companies. Look for it in flaked form.

Castile soap. An important ingredient, castile soap is sold at health food stores, in some supermarkets, and via mail order.

Citrus seed extract. Usually made from grapefruit seed, this natural preservative is a powerful antimicrobial agent. It is typically sold in capsule form as grapefruit seed extract, also known as ParaMicrocidin, and is available online and at some health food stores.

Cream of tartar. A popular culinary ingredient, this powdered mixture is sold in a box in the herb and spice or baking aisle of any supermarket.

Diatomaceous earth. This powder, made from the skeletons of fossilized algae, is available at garden supply and hardware stores, as well as through mail-order companies. Note, however, that this type of food-grade diatomaceous earth is not the same substance that you can buy from pool supply centers.

Essential oils. These concentrated volatile oils of plants can be found at health food stores and specialty shops and via mail order.

Glycerin. Glycerin is a useful liquid for cleaners, medicines, and even some craft projects. You'll find it at art and craft stores, some pharmacies, and natural food stores.

Lanolin. Lanolin, an oily substance derived from sheep's wool, can be purchased from mail-order companies.

Murphy's Oil Soap. A very popular liquid soap for wood, Murphy's is sold at just about any supermarket. Check the cleaning products aisle.

Soap flakes. Order online or buy pure castile soap at the health food store and grate it yourself.

Washing soda. Washing soda's generic name is sodium carbonate, and it's also known as soda ash. Some supermarkets stock Arm & Hammer Super Washing Soda in the laundry products aisle. If yours doesn't, you can purchase it online.

White vinegar. Used in many cuisines, white vinegar is found in the oil aisle of any supermarket.

SUGGESTED EQUIPMENT

Many of these implements may already be on hand. Wash and rinse the containers from your old products and they're ready to service you again in your nontoxic cleaning chores. Be sure to label your product with a list of ingredients; any type of label from an office supply, stationery, or grocery store will do. While you're at it, be creative and give your formula a catchy name! Since labels can get wet, they are best covered with clear shipping tape or laminating sheets cut to size. Plan to keep the following around:

Spray bottles. Get both small and large sizes.

Containers with shaker tops. Spice containers are great.

Misters (glass pump spray bottles).

Coffee cans with lids. These are great for storing waxes and pastes.

Glass jars. Preferably get wide-mouthed jars with screw-top lids.

Cotton cloths. When possible, use cloths instead of paper towels.

Rags. T-shirts, scrap cotton cloth, and old towels are examples of good rags for cleaning.

Cellulose sponge cloth. Made of natural cellulose, these are absorbent, nonscratching, washable, and durable.

Gallon buckets. For large jobs.

Mops. Use a cotton-head mop for floors and a sponge-head mop for carpets and walls.

MAKING A STARTER KIT

The following essential oils are inexpensive, readily available, and the most effective in cleaning formulas and are recommended throughout this book. You are not held hostage to this list or any particular essential oil on it. In fact, you're encouraged to experiment and make substitutions when necessary. But keep in mind that certain cleaning formulas may recommend using tea tree over sweet orange, for example, because the former contains specific properties. See the chart on page 16 for guidance.

* Lavender
* Peppermint
* Rosemary
* Sage

* Sweet orange
* Tea tree
* Thyme

Essential Oils and Their Properties

A great number of plants contain volatile compounds with antibacterial, antifungal, and/or antiviral properties. The list on the next page is by no means complete, but it represents some of the more commonly available essential oils that are effective and that won't break the bank.

ESSENTIAL OIL	PROPERTIES
Cinnamon	antiviral
Citronella	antibacterial
Clove	antibiotic, antiviral
Cypress	antibacterial
Eucalyptus	antibiotic, antifungal, antiviral, antibacterial
Ginger	antibacterial
Lavender	antibiotic, antifungal, antiviral, antibacterial
Lemon	antibiotic, antifungal, antiviral, antibacterial
Lemongrass	antibacterial
Lime	antibiotic, antibacterial
Marjoram	antibacterial
Nutmeg	antibiotic
Sweet orange	antibacterial
Oregano	antibiotic, antiviral
Pine	antibiotic, antibacterial
Rosemary	antibacterial
Sage	antifungal, antibacterial
Spearmint	antibacterial
Tea tree	antibiotic, antifungal, antiviral, antibacterial
Thyme	antibiotic, antifungal, antiviral
Wintergreen	antibacterial (take extra care when handling)

CHAPTER 2

THE KITCHEN

TO ME, THE KITCHEN IS THE HUB AND HEART OF A HOME. This room is more than a storage receptacle for culinary sundries; it's where we gather with cherished family and friends for mealtime celebrations. Unfortunately, it's also the room where the garbage is usually kept, where a bare floor endures the patter of muddy feet, and where the odor of grease and last night's fish stubbornly linger. In other words, it's a haven for germs. Save for the loo, the kitchen is probably the most frequented room in the house and is most in need of daily cleaning.

It's a pity that most of us grew up to think a clean kitchen is only evidenced by the overwhelming and pungent smell of a pine solvent. And little did we realize that our nervous systems were being treated to an assault of toxins. But you can create your own cost-effective, healthy alternatives to all the kitchen cleaners you're accustomed to using.

Washing the Dishes

Dishwashing liquids and automatic dishwasher detergents have been designed to lure the consumer with their stimulating lemony scent. Their aromatic choice is more than an advertising gimmick; sure, citrus oils smell nice, but they are also natural degreasers. It's the rest of the ingredients in these harsh detergents that we are better off without.

DISHWASHING LIQUIDS

The herbal essential oils recommended in the following formulas will pack a punch on germs and greasy dirt without knocking you out in the process.

Fruity Dishwashing Blend

This blend will have you looking forward to washing dishes!

> liquid castile soap
> 15 drops lemon or lemongrass essential oil
> 6 drops lavender essential oil
> 5 drops bergamot essential oil

Fill a clean 22-ounce squirt bottle with castile soap (diluted according to directions if using concentrate). Add the essential oils. Shake the bottle before each use. Add 1 to 2 tablespoons of the liquid to dishwater and wash as usual.

Citrus Dishwashing Blend

Here's another sweet-smelling formula.

	liquid castile soap
20	drops lime essential oil
10	drops sweet orange essential oil
5	drops citrus seed extract

Fill a clean 22-ounce squirt bottle with castile soap (diluted according to directions if using concentrate). Add the essential oils and extract. Shake the bottle before each use. Add 1 to 2 tablespoons of the liquid to dishwater and wash as usual.

Herbal Dishwashing Blend

Enjoy the leafy-fresh fragrance as you wash!

	liquid castile soap
10	drops lavender essential oil
8	drops rosemary essential oil
4	drops eucalyptus essential oil

Fill a clean 22-ounce squirt bottle with castile soap (diluted according to directions if using concentrate). Add the essential oils. Shake the bottle before each use. Add 1 to 2 tablespoons of the liquid to dishwater and wash as usual.

Dishwashing Blues Blend

Try this recipe for an uplifting washing experience.

liquid castile soap

10 drops lemon essential oil

6 drops bergamot essential oil

4 drops lavender essential oil

2 drops orange essential oil

Fill a clean 22-ounce squirt bottle with castile soap (diluted according to directions if using concentrate). Add the essential oils. Shake the bottle before each use. Add 1 to 2 tablespoons of the liquid to dishwater and wash as usual.

DON'T GIVE UP ON THE TOUGH JOBS

* For very greasy dishes, add ½ cup vinegar or lemon juice to the dishwater.
* To loosen baked-on food from pots and pans, sprinkle baking soda on them immediately after cooking and wait 15 minutes before cleaning. If the pot or pan has cooled before you've had a chance to add baking soda, boil a solution of 1 cup water, 5 drops of cedar or other essential oil, and 3 tablespoons baking soda directly in the pot or pan. Allow the mixture to stand until the food can be scraped off easily.

AUTOMATIC DISHWASHER DETERGENTS

Here are several easy-to-make formulas for your automatic dishwasher that will get the job done for just pennies per load. Citric acid is available in powdered form from many health food stores, stores that cater to homebrewers of beer and wine, soapmaking supply outlets and, of course, from various online sources. It is sometimes labeled as "sour salt."

Lavender Lift Automatic Dishwasher Powder

Enjoy the subtle fragrance of this formula while your dishes are being cleaned.

 1 **cup washing soda**
 1 **cup baking soda**
 1 **cup salt**
 ½ **cup citric acid powder**
 20 **drops lavender**
    essential oil

Combine the washing soda, baking soda, salt, and citric acid powder in a container with a lid. Stir in the essential oil. Cover and store in a dry place. Use 1 tablespoon per load of dishes.

Citrus Sparkle Automatic Dishwasher Powder

This formula is the same as Lavender Lift (page 21) but uses sweet orange essential oil for a fresh citrus scent.

- 1 **cup washing soda**
- 1 **cup baking soda**
- 1 **cup salt**
- ½ **cup citric acid powder**
- 20 **drops sweet orange or other citrus essential oil**

Combine the washing soda, baking soda, salt, and citric acid powder in a container with a lid. Stir in the essential oil. Store covered in a dry place. Use 1 tablespoon per load of dishes.

Homemade Dishwasher Tablets

These tablets are actually fun to make and offer an easy grab-and-go alternative to measuring a powdered mix. You can purchase molds online made for this purpose, or you can simply use an ice cube tray.

- 1 **cup washing soda**
- 1 **cup baking soda**
- 1 **cup Epsom salts**
- ½ **cup citric acid powder**
- 1 **cup water**
- 20 **drops lemon or lime essential oil**

1. Combine the washing soda, baking soda, Epsom salts, and citric acid powder in a large glass or ceramic bowl.
2. In a separate small bowl, stir together the water and essential oil. (They won't mix completely, but that's okay. The water is just a vehicle for the oil.) Slowly add the liquid to the dry mix. When the mixture stops fizzing, stir until well combined.
3. Working quickly, fill the molds with the mixture and press down with the back of a spoon to make each one as compact as possible so they'll hold together. Set aside for 30 to 45 minutes before turning the tablets out onto a dry surface.
4. Let the tablets harden for a few hours before storing in a clean container with a lid. Use 1 tablet per load of dishes.

Rescue Rinse for Hard Water

If you frequently find spots on your glasses or flatware, then you might want to try this simple remedy:

2 tablespoons white distilled vinegar

Add the vinegar to the rinse compartment of your dishwasher.

Tea Time for Two

Tea contains tannic acid, which will help break down and remove soap residue from your dishes during the rinse cycle.

2 cups green or white tea, freshly brewed

Add one cup to the rinse compartment of your dishwasher, then relax while sipping the remaining cup.

Dishwasher Cleaner

Gunk and grime can build up in your dishwasher over time, resulting in reduced performance. Treat your machine to this simple cleaning solution, ideally once a month.

- **1 cup distilled vinegar**
- **5 drops tea tree essential oil**
- **5 drops sage essential oil**

Combine all ingredients in a small glass bowl or cup. Place right-side up in the top rack of the empty dishwasher and run the regular cycle.

The Kitchen Sink

The baking soda–essential oil mixtures in the following formulas can be made in larger batches and stored in a container, glass jar, or coffee can (store the vinegar separately). I find the large spice and herb jars with shaker tops are perfect for powdered cleaners. Just soak off the label and wash and dry the inside of the container.

Basic Sink Cleanser

This formula is safe for porcelain or stainless steel sinks. Not only will it clean the sink basin and faucets, but it will also keep drains and garbage disposals fresh smelling and free of clogs. Note: A vinegar rinse can be used before the final hot-water rinse to prevent residue from the baking soda.

- ¼ **cup baking soda**
- ¼ **cup vinegar**
- 3 **drops lavender, rosemary, lemon, lime, or sweet orange essential oil**

Combine all ingredients in a large bowl. Rinse the sink well with hot water. Pour the cleanser in the sink and wipe with a sponge or cloth. Rinse again with hot water.

Sage Scrubber

Baking soda lends a scratch-proof grit to this scrubber to safely clean surfaces, while sage essential oil provides antimicrobial and antifungal properties. Sage is also a potent deodorizer, making this formula idea for kitchen sinks and drains.

- 1 **cup baking soda**
- 15 **drops sage essential oil**

Combine the baking soda and essential oil in an airtight container and shake well to blend. Sprinkle a small amount of the powder into the sink and scrub with a damp sponge. Rinse well.

Country Spice Scrubber

Simple and sweet!

- **1 cup baking soda**
- **3 teaspoons ground cinnamon**
- **3 drops cedar or sweet orange essential oil**

Combine all ingredients in an airtight container and shake well to blend. Sprinkle a small amount of the powder into the sink and scrub with a damp sponge. Rinse well.

Sink Scrubber for Stains

For stubborn stains, allow this formula to rest on the stain for several minutes. Then scrub and rinse with vinegar and hot water.

- **¼ cup Epsom salts**
- **¼ cup baking soda**
- **8 drops rosemary, eucalyptus, or tea tree essential oil**
- **¾ cup vinegar for rinsing**

Combine the Epsom salts, baking soda, and essential oil in an airtight container and shake well to blend. Sprinkle a small amount of the powder into the sink and scrub with a damp sponge. Rinse the sink with the vinegar, then with hot water.

SIMPLE SINK CLEANSER

Bon Ami brand cleanser is made of grated detergent and feldspar and is nontoxic and nonabrasive. Sprinkle it freely in the sink basin and add 5 or 6 drops of essential oil of choice, if desired. Scrub and rinse well.

Porcelain Sink Saver

Old-fashioned porcelain tubs and sinks offer lovely rustic charm, but they can take on scuff marks and stains rather easily. This scouring formula gets assistance from powdered pumice (volcanic rock) to help restore their beauty — and it works well as a cleanser for hardworking hands to boot! Note: Not recommended for use on fiberglass.

- ½ **cup baking soda**
- ½ **cup pumice powder**
- 2 **tablespoons citric acid powder**
- 2 **tablespoons liquid castile soap**
- 1 **teaspoon sweet orange essential oil**

Combine all ingredients in a small bowl. Scoop into a small glass jar or tin with a tight-fitting lid. To use, apply a small amount to surfaces with a damp cloth or sponge, and rub using a circular motion. Rinse well with hot water. If the mixture becomes too pasty, thin with a bit of warm water.

Rust Remover

Wipe away these unattractive stains with a fresh-scented cleaner. Note: If the stain is on the side of your sink, use more baking soda to make a thick paste that will cling to the spot.

¼ cup baking soda
5 drops essential oil of choice
   juice of half a lemon

Sprinkle the baking soda directly on the rust stain. Add the essential oil and sprinkle with lemon juice. Allow the mixture to sit on the stain undisturbed for several hours or overnight. Wipe away the baking soda and rinse thoroughly.

Oven Cleaners

Commercial oven cleaners are one of the most toxic and unpleasant products you could use. If the fumes from the application aren't bad enough, the foul smell of chemical burn-off the stuff continues to produce is enough to make one afraid of turning on the oven! The following formulas work very well. No oven cleaner is a miracle worker, however. Sometimes it may require a bit of elbow grease if there's a great deal of buildup on your oven walls and floor.

When vinegar is added to baking soda, a fizzing reaction occurs. While this might startle you at first, it is perfectly normal.

SOAK THOSE STOVE ACCESSORIES!

The chrome rings that surround burners on an electric stove, the grills that rest on gas stove burners, and oven knobs all collect grease and food splatters over time. While cleaning your oven, soak these items in a solution of 1 cup baking soda, ½ cup vinegar, and 4 to 6 drops of essential oil of your choice. Use a fine steel wool pad or old toothbrush to remove grime from small spaces.

Serious Oven-Cleaning Formula

I once made a family-size turkey pot pie in one of my best crocks and watched helplessly as it began bubbling over within minutes of putting it in the oven. What a mess! This formula is great for such disasters, or for ovens that have been neglected for a while. Note: If you have a lot of baked-on grease or food splatters, you may want to use fine steel wool to scrub those areas. Use a bit more salt if necessary.

½ cup salt

¼ cup washing soda

1 (16-ounce) box baking soda

water

¾ cup white vinegar

10 drops thyme essential oil

10 drops lemon or lemongrass essential oil

1. Combine the salt, washing soda, and baking soda in a container or glass bowl. Add just enough water (a scant ¼ cup) to make a paste.

2. Remove the oven racks and preheat the oven to 250°F/120°C for 15 minutes, then turn off the oven and leave the door open.

3. Carefully spread the paste on the oven walls with a sponge or cloth and allow to set for 20 to 30 minutes.

4. Combine the vinegar and essential oils in a spray bottle and shake well. Spray the oven walls and wipe clean. Rinse well.

Overnight Oven Cleaner

Bring out these proven grease-cutting oils for those heavy-duty oven-cleaning jobs.

1 **cup water**

10 **drops sweet orange, lemon, or rosemary essential oil**

½ **cup salt**

1¼ **cups baking soda**

2 **teaspoons liquid castile soap**

¼ **cup vinegar**

1. Block the vents in the oven floor with aluminum foil or waxed paper. Preheat the oven to 300°F/150°C for 15 minutes, then turn off the oven and leave the door open.

2. Combine ¼ cup of the water with the essential oil in a spray bottle and shake well. Spray the oven floor and walls with this precleaning mixture.

3. Combine ¼ cup of the salt and ½ cup of the baking soda. Sprinkle the mixture on the oven floor, paying particular attention to spill areas.

4. Mix ¼ cup of the water with the remaining ¾ cup baking soda, the remaining ¼ cup salt, and the castile soap. Spread this mixture on the oven walls. Remove the foil or waxed paper from the vents and allow the paste to sit overnight.

5. In the morning, combine the remaining ½ cup water with the vinegar in a spray bottle. Spray the oven walls and floor generously with this mixture. Wipe well, using fine steel wool to work off any stubborn spots. Rinse several times to remove any residue.

Sunday Oven-Cleaning Formula

This formula is for regular oven maintenance.

> 2 tablespoons baking soda
>
> 2 tablespoons liquid castile soap
>
> 10 drops sweet orange, lemon, or lime essential oil
>
> ½ cup hot water

1. Preheat the oven to 250°F/120°C for 15 minutes, then turn off and leave the door open.
2. Combine the baking soda, castile soap, and essential oil in a clean spray bottle. Add the water and shake well.
3. Spray on the oven walls and wait 20 minutes. Wipe clean and rinse well.

KEEP THOSE CABINETS SPARKLING

If you have plastic laminate cabinets in your kitchen, you can clean them with an all-purpose cleaner such as any of the formulas in this section. The kitchen cabinets in our home are made of oak; for these I use a mixture of 2 cups water, ¼ cup Murphy's Oil Soap, and 15 to 20 drops of cedar or patchouli essential oil. The scent is heavenly — clean and woodlike.

Cleaning Kitchen Surfaces

Kitchen appliances, such as refrigerators, microwave ovens, and dishwashers, can get grimy from cooking grease and odors. Let's not forget those little fingerprints that magically appear on cabinet doors! The following formulas will clean without scratching surfaces, and they can be made in larger batches and stored in spray bottles.

Lemon Blast Cleaner

This solution is great for refrigerators and stovetops.

1 teaspoon liquid castile soap

⅛ cup white vinegar

¼ cup lemon juice

2 cups water

6 drops citrus seed extract

4 drops lemon, lime, orange, or eucalyptus essential oil

1 teaspoon baking soda

Combine all ingredients in a spray bottle. Shake well before each use. Spray generously on the appliance surface and wipe with a damp cloth or sponge. Wipe dry with a cloth or towel.

Herbal Degreaser

This formula will remove greasy film from appliance surfaces.

  2 cups water
  ¼ cup oil-based soap (Murphy's is good)
  10 drops rosemary, lavender, or citrus essential oil

Combine all ingredients in a spray bottle. Shake well before each use. Spray generously on the appliance surface and wipe with a damp cloth or sponge. Wipe dry with a cloth or towel.

Just in Thyme Sani-Spray

Sometimes things that land on kitchen surfaces — like raw poultry or egg — can leave behind dangerous microorganisms. Keep this go-to spray under the sink so it's on hand when needed.

  2 cups hot water
  ¼ cup distilled white vinegar
  ½ teaspoon washing soda
  20 drops thyme essential oil
  10 drops lavender essential oil

Combine all ingredients in a spray bottle and shake well. To use, shake the bottle and spray the solution on surfaces. Wait 1 to 2 minutes before wiping with a dry cloth.

Gentle Granite Cleanser

Acidic substances, like vinegar or citrus, can cause pitting and erosion of the finish on granite countertops. For the most part, all that is needed to clean granite is a warm, soapy cloth. However, although granite is nonporous, there may be times when you'd like to eliminate the risk of bacteria lingering on the surface. Here's a simple rescue formula for those occasions. As an added bonus, the use of clove, cinnamon leaf, or peppermint essential oil in this formula not only kills germs but also deters flies, ants, and other kitchen pests by blocking an insect neurotransmitter called octopamine and interfering with their metabolism, heart rate, and central nervous system. People and animals, however, are not affected because they lack octopamine receptors.

- 2 cups distilled water
- ¼ cup 91% isopropyl alcohol
- 5 drops liquid castile soap
- 15 drops clove essential oil

Combine all ingredients in a spray bottle and shake well. Shake the bottle gently before each use. Spray on surfaces and wipe the cleaner off with a dry, soft cloth.

Lavender Stainless Steel Cleanser

Stainless steel appliances can get easily streaked and smeared. This cleanser will shine them right up.

- ½ cup distilled vinegar
- ½ cup 91% isopropyl alcohol
- 15 drops lavender essential oil

Combine all ingredients in a spray bottle. Shake gently before each use. Spray on surfaces and wipe with a dry, lint-free cloth.

Microwave Cleaner

The interior of a microwave oven can trap grease and cooking odors that can spoil the flavor of foods during cooking. Try this remedy whenever you think your microwave could use a little sprucing up. If your microwave has a glass turntable, remove it and wash it by hand.

¼ cup baking soda

1 teaspoon vinegar

5–6 drops thyme, lemongrass, or lemon essential oil

Combine all ingredients in a bowl to make a paste. Apply to the walls and floor of the microwave with a soft cloth or sponge. Rinse well and leave the microwave door open to air-dry for about 25 minutes.

Citrus Pot Scrubber

Cooking over a gas flame can sometimes leave black marks on the bottoms of your pots and pans. Keep this scrubber handy for such occasions.

1 cup baking soda

10 drops sweet orange, lime, or lemon essential oil

distilled vinegar, as needed

Combine the baking soda and essential oil in a small bowl. Transfer into a small glass jar or tin with a tight-fitting lid and store in a dry place. To use, sprinkle a small amount over the item and scrub with a damp cloth or sponge. Rinse well with hot water. *Note:* For stubborn stains, add a small amount of

vinegar over the powder until it fizzes, then let the item soak
for several minutes before proceeding.

Refrigerator & Freezer Rescue

We all have the best of intentions when we pack away
those little containers of leftover foods and store
them in the refrigerator. But often these receptacles
are forgotten, and the telltale aroma of something
well past its prime soon makes its presence known,
just a bit too late. Odors due to expired foods, or
even up-to-date pungent-smelling foods (like some
cheeses), can create an offensive smell noticeable
whenever the refrigerator door is opened. Strong
odors can also affect fresh foods in both the refrigerator and the freezer.

If an unfriendly fragrance has permeated your
freezer, remove all the contents and put them on
ice in a cooler temporarily. If you have a separate
temperature control for the freezer, turn it down
for a few minutes to warm the freezer up a little. (If
there isn't a separate control, leave the freezer door
open for 5 minutes.) Wipe the interior of the freezer
with a soft cloth dampened with a solution of ½ cup
water, 3 tablespoons baking soda, and 6 drops of
eucalyptus or peppermint essential oil. Rinse well to
remove any baking soda residue, and dry the walls,
shelves, and floor of the freezer thoroughly with a tea

towel before replacing the food. Don't forget to turn the temperature-control setting back up!

For refrigerator odors, you can use the same solution to wipe down the walls, shelves, and doors, but increase the amount of essential oil to 10 drops.

MAINTAINING FRESHNESS

If you just want to maintain freshness in the refrigerator, try one of these scented solutions:

Vanilla. Pour 2 ounces vanilla extract (imitation is okay) into a small, shallow bowl or saucer and place it on a lower shelf for a few days.

Coffee. If you like the smell of coffee, place a bowl of ½ cup ground coffee on a shelf. This will last for several weeks. You can add 5 to 7 drops of essential oil or even ground herbs, such as vanilla bean, sarsaparilla, mace, or ginger.

If you have a persistent odor in the refrigerator, try one of these tips:

Citrus. Line the bottom shelf with newspaper that has been sprinkled with 10 to 15 drops of essential oil, such as lemon, lime, grapefruit, or sweet orange. Remove after 2 or 3 days.

Herb. If you have an herb garden currently in bloom, cut a few stems of fragrant plants such as sage, rosemary, lemon balm, or mint. Tie with string and hang from one of the racks. The fresh herbs should last for 2 to 3 weeks.

Unscented. A slice of bread left on a plate will absorb many odors. You can sprinkle the bread slice with 2 to 4 drops of essential oil of your choice for extra deodorizing power.

CONTROLLING KITCHEN PESTS

Even the cleanest kitchens are susceptible to unwanted visitors. Give bugs the boot with these quick remedies.

Ants. Wipe out your kitchen cabinets with a damp sponge and 6 to 8 drops of peppermint or citronella essential oil. Then place 3 to 5 drops of those essential oils on windowsills, in doorway cracks, and in the corners of the cabinet under your kitchen sink.

Centipedes, earwigs, and silverfish. Place several drops of peppermint, wintergreen, eucalyptus, or citronella essential oil in areas that collect moisture, such as damp basements, garages, and cabinets that house plumbing fixtures.

Cockroaches. Sprinkle a mixture of food-grade diatomaceous earth and sugar in the dark areas where roaches like to hide. *Note:* This method might not be feasible if you have young children or pets. It may be best to consult an exterminator.

Mice. Place several sprigs of fresh peppermint between pantry items in your cabinets, or make a solution of 2 cups water and 3 teaspoons peppermint essential oil and spray it wherever you find mouse droppings.

Mites and weevils. Place a few whole nutmegs in flour bins or bags. .

Other insects. Place loose bay leaves in your kitchen cabinets.

The Kitchen Floor

Our family has trampled on several different kinds of flooring over the years, from white tile (who does this in a kitchen?) to the 200-year-old wide-plank hemlock flooring in the home that we currently occupy. Although the children have fled the nest and all the fur-kids have crossed the bridge, my husband and I still manage to make a mess on our own. Then there are grandchildren, "grand-pups," and other canines that accompany visiting friends. It's a blessing and a joy whenever our cherished loved ones find their way home to us. Dirt? Not so much.

The type of cleaner to use on your kitchen floor will depend on the type of flooring you have, as well as the foot traffic. While all of the formulas suggested here are effective and safe for people and pets, you should avoid the use of white vinegar if you have hardwood or no-wax floors because its acidity may damage the finish over time. This is also true for stone surfaces.

GET RID OF SCUFF MARKS
To remove scuff marks, apply 2 to 4 drops of essential oil neat (undiluted) and wipe clean with a cloth. Rinse with a dash of vinegar.

Pine-Fresh Floor Cleaner

This formula isn't at all like the old pine-solvent cleaners you may be used to. It works just as well but leaves a light scent more reminiscent of a pine forest than a bucket of chemicals. You can adjust the scent to your preference by increasing or reducing the amount of essential oil used.

1 gallon hot water

2 tablespoons liquid castile soap

10 drops pine essential oil

5 drops cypress essential oil

Combine all ingredients in a large bucket. Dip a mop into the bucket and squeeze out excess liquid. Clean the floor by working in sections, using short strokes and dipping the mop as needed. Rinsing is not necessary.

Citrus Floor Cleaner

Nothing works like citrus in the kitchen!

1 gallon hot water

2 tablespoons liquid castile soap

15 drops sweet orange essential oil

8 drops lemon essential oil, or ¼ cup lemon juice

Combine all ingredients in a large bucket. Dip a mop into the bucket and squeeze out excess liquid. Clean the floor by working in sections, using short strokes and dipping the mop as needed. Rinsing is not necessary.

Tough Dirt & Grease Formula

Put the grease–cutting power of vinegar to use with this excellent formula.

- 1 **gallon hot water**
- 2 **tablespoons liquid castile soap**
- ¼ **cup washing soda**
- 1 **cup vinegar**
- 20 **drops eucalyptus, peppermint, or tea tree essential oil**

Combine all ingredients in a large bucket. Dip a mop into the bucket and squeeze out excess liquid. Clean the floor by working in sections, using short strokes and dipping the mop as needed. Rinsing is not necessary.

FLOOR WIPES

Cleaning wipes designed to fit electrostatic mops for cleaning floors have become very popular in recent years, rendering the traditional mop and bucket obsolete. Successfully creating your own floor wipes depends on using the right materials to make the wipes from, as well as storing them properly to keep them from drying out.

To make the wipes more environmentally friendly, use cellulose cloth cut to size. Cellulose is a sturdy material made from tree fibers and is free of petrochemicals. It's also completely biodegradable, unlike typical store-bought wipes. Your best bet for locating a source for this material (and, hopefully, one that makes use of a renewable tree farm) is with an internet search. Larger-size cloths come in rolls like paper towels.

There are various ways you can store your pre-treated floor wipes — stacked in an airtight container, coiled in a can, or simply folded and sealed in a zip-lock bag. Whatever option you choose, your storage container will be reusable.

Use your homemade floor wipes on tile, lino-leum, or sealed wood floors.

Rosemary-Geranium Floor Wipes

These fragrant wipes will almost make cleaning the floor a pleasure.

1 **cup water**
1 **cup white vinegar**
10 **drops rosemary essential oil**
10 **drops geranium essential oil**

Mix all ingredients in a bowl. Stack your precut wipes on top of each other (or roll them together jelly roll–style if you're going to coil the wipes to store them) and place them in the bowl with the cleaning solution. Allow the wipes to absorb the liquid for a few moments. Immediately transfer the wipes to your storage container of choice, together with about ¼ cup of the liquid to keep them moist, and seal.

The Bee's Knees Floor Wipes

The botanical ingredients used in this formula will remind you of a clover-covered knoll. Hint: Purchasing a combination of dried red clover flowers and leaves is less expensive than buying the blossoms in bulk.

- 2 **teaspoons dried red clover flowers and/or leaves**
- ½ **cup boiling water**
- 1 **cup white vinegar**
- 10 **drops grapefruit seed extract**

Brew a tea by placing the red clover into a bowl. Pour the boiled water over the herb and steep for 10 minutes, then strain. When the tea has cooled, add the remaining ingredients and blend. Soak the precut wipes in this mixture for a few minutes, then store. Add just enough of the cleaning solution to the storage container to keep the wipes moist.

HELPFUL HINTS FOR THE KITCHEN

Wipe up food spills in the oven as soon as possible. Better yet, line your oven with aluminum foil to prevent spills from caking on in the first place. Enamel stovetops can sometimes get those hard-to-wipe-off stains that only get worse as time goes on. But if you sprinkle on a few drops of your favorite essential oil, the stain will wipe clean.

Sprinkle fresh grease spills in the oven with salt. When the oven has cooled, wipe clean with a soft cloth. Baking soda will also soak up the grease when applied this way.

Sanitize wooden cutting boards by rubbing with half of a freshly cut lemon, lime, or grapefruit. Or soak the board in a solution of 2 cups water and 15 drops of a citrus essential oil. Then wash with a mild soap and hot water.

Electric can openers can collect a lot of gunk. Who wants to open a can of tuna for lunch after opening Fluffy and Fido's dinner the night before? Use an old, soft toothbrush dampened with 2 or 3 drops of any essential oil to clean in and between those small parts. Rinse, and the gunk is gone.

Keep garbage disposals smelling fresh by tossing in the remains of a lemon, grapefruit, or lime when available.

How about some ready-when-you-need-'em kitchen wipes? Instead of using paper towels to wipe up spills or clean off countertops, store multiple squares of soft cotton cloth or cellulose sponge in a container filled with a mixture of 1 cup water, 1 ounce liquid castile soap, and 6 to 8 drops of your favorite essential oil. The cloths, made from old T-shirts or pajamas, can be washed and returned to the jar for reuse. Be sure to cap the jar between uses.

Keep a supply of 100 percent cotton cloths and towels on hand to use instead of paper towels.

Use cloth napkins and placemats whenever possible to reduce your consumption of paper napkins.

Storage containers can get heavily stained from foods such as tomato sauce, especially if they're frequently microwaved to reheat leftovers. For these stains, let the containers soak in a strong infusion of fresh lemon balm, mint, or sage, with a tablespoon of baking soda. After soaking for an hour or so, scrub the container with a little more baking soda if needed. The stains may not disappear entirely, but they're bound to look better than before.

Reduce your use of plastic wrap, aluminum foil, and brown paper bags by using glass containers or special metal containers known as bentos to tote lunches to work or school. Sturdy straws made from gluten-free wheat stalks and utensils made from sustainable bamboo can replace plasticware and plastic straws. If you already have a cupboard full of plastic containers, consider retiring them from kitchen service and giving them new life as storage containers in the garage, workshop, or craft room. Of course, you can also check with your recycling provider to see if they accept them.

THE BATH

THE BATHROOM IS A BREEDING GROUND FOR GERMS, due
to the nature of things we do there. Other than the
obvious activities, there's also a lot of hair brushing,
sloughing of dry skin, and plenty of body-care rituals
with the potential for making mold and mildew. If you
have more than one bathroom, there's more of the
same going on there. These formulas are gentle on your
hands and get the job done without harmful chemicals.

Mold & Mildew Busters

Mold and mildew are always a threat, especially if there is a window with a sill in your bathroom. The steam from showers and baths can affect the woodwork of the window and lead to peeling paint and mildew spots. Ventilation, such as an exhaust fan, can help minimize this problem.

The same applies to the shower curtain. The best kind of shower curtain to buy is a cloth type that can be laundered. Hang it to dry in the sun to thwart mildew and bacteria.

Knock 'Em Dead Thyme Disinfectant Spray

Thymol, the compound responsible for the spicy flavor of common thyme (Thymus vulgaris) *also has antiseptic, antibacterial, and antifungal properties. The essential oil of thyme contains a concentration of up to 54 percent thymol.*

- 2 cups hot water
- 25 drops thyme essential oil
- 2 teaspoons citric acid powder

Combine all ingredients in a spray bottle and shake well. Shake before each use. Spray on surfaces and wipe clean with a damp cloth or sponge.

Pine Disinfectant

You'll definitely prefer this recipe to your old pine cleaner!

- 2 **cups water**
- 2 **teaspoons washing soda**
- 8 **drops pine essential oil**
- 4 **drops cedar essential oil**

Combine all ingredients in a spray bottle. Shake before each use. Spray on surfaces and wipe clean with a damp cloth or sponge.

Mold & Mildew Prevention Formula

Use this formula on shower stalls and curtains, the tracks between sliding glass doors, and in other moist areas.

- 2 **cups water**
- 8–10 **drops citrus seed extract**
- 2 **teaspoons tea tree essential oil**
- 4 **drops juniper essential oil**

Combine all ingredients in a spray bottle. Spray areas and surfaces well but do not rinse. *Note:* If you already have a buildup of mold or mildew, allow the spray to rest on the surface areas for a few hours. Wipe with a soft cloth, then respray the areas and let dry without rinsing.

Mold Deterrent

If you already have a buildup of mold or mildew, allow the spray to rest on the surface areas for a few hours. Wipe with a soft cloth, then respray the areas and let dry without rinsing.

- 1¼ cups white vinegar
- ¾ cup water
- 4 drops cinnamon essential oil
- 6 drops clove essential oil
- 2 teaspoons tea tree essential oil

Combine all ingredients in a spray bottle. Spray surfaces well but do not rinse.

Minty Mirror Magic

This mixture not only cleans the mirror (and faucets) to a shine, but it will help prevent fogging while the shower is running.

- 1½ cups vinegar
- ½ cup water
- 8 drops peppermint essential oil

Combine all ingredients in a spray bottle and shake well before use. Spray the solution onto the mirror and wipe with a dry cloth or towel.

Scouring Powders & Cleansers

The following cleaners possess sanitizing and antibacterial qualities while offering a variety of herbal scents. You can make larger batches of these products and store them in containers. (Large spice jars with shaker tops work great for this purpose.)

Herbal Scouring Powder for Sinks

This powder rubs out grime while leaving a fresh, earthy scent. Make sure you rinse well to remove any residue.

- 1 cup baking soda
- ¼ cup citric acid powder
- 1 teaspoon cream of tartar
- 15 drops lavender or sweet orange essential oil

Combine all ingredients in a container, preferably one with a shaker top. Shake well. Sprinkle a small amount of the powder into the sink and scrub with a damp sponge or cloth. Rinse well with plain water.

CLEANING FAUCETS

The best thing for cleaning bathroom faucets is a simple mixture of equal parts water and vinegar. If you have a buildup of grime around the base of the faucet, put 3 or 4 drops of a citrus essential oil directly on the dirt, then clean with a toothbrush. Great for kitchen faucets, too!

Whitening Scouring Powder

The combination of washing soda and orange essential oil will remove stains and kill germs.

- 1 **cup baking soda**
- ½ **cup washing soda**
- 2 **teaspoons cream of tartar**
- 20 **drops sweet orange essential oil**

Combine all ingredients in a container, preferably one with a shaker top. Shake well. Sprinkle a small amount of the powder into the sink, and scrub with a damp sponge or cloth. Rinse well.

Lemony Scouring Powder

This formula is for lemon lovers!

- 1 **cup baking soda**
- ½ **cup pumice powder**
- 25 **drops lemon essential oil**

Combine all ingredients in a container, preferably one with a shaker top. Shake well. Sprinkle the powder onto surfaces and scrub with a damp cloth or sponge. Rinse well.

Earthy Scouring Powder

This cleanser will make you think you're tending your garden instead of cleaning the bathroom.

- 1 cup baking soda
- ½ cup pumice powder
- 5 drops rosemary essential oil
- 5 drops lavender essential oil
- 5 drops thyme essential oil

Combine all ingredients in a container, preferably one with a shaker top. Shake well. Sprinkle the powder onto surfaces and scrub with a damp cloth or sponge. Rinse well.

Tub & Tile Soft Scrubber

A small mason jar or jelly jar is ideal for storing soft scrubber.

- 1 cup baking soda
- ¼ cup liquid castile soap
- 2 vitamin C tablets, crushed
- 3–5 drops eucalyptus or tea tree essential oil
- water

Combine the baking soda, castile soap, vitamin C, and essential oil in a bottle. Add just enough water to make a smooth liquid paste. Shake or stir to mix. Apply the paste to surfaces and rub with a damp cloth or sponge until the area is clean. Rinse several times with water.

Lavender Soft Scrubber

This scrubber not only cleans, but is mild and will actually soften your hands!

- ¾ cup baking soda
- ¼ cup powdered milk
- ⅛ cup liquid castile soap
- 5 drops lavender essential oil
- water

Combine the baking soda, milk, castile soap, and essential oil in a squeeze bottle. Add just enough water to make a smooth paste. Shake or stir to mix. Apply to surfaces, then wipe the area clean with a damp sponge or cloth. Rinse well.

Lime Scale Remover

If you have well water, then you're probably familiar — and frustrated — with lime scale. Use this formula as both a remedy and a deterrent on shower walls and doors.

- 1 cup liquid castile soap
- 1 cup distilled vinegar
- 15 drops tea tree essential oil
- 15 drops lemon essential oil

Combine all ingredients in a spray bottle. Shake well before each use. Spray on surfaces and let rest for several minutes before rinsing with hot water.

Grout Cleaner

Use this formula to brighten dirty tile grout. This is why we save old toothbrushes!

- **2** cups boiling water
- **½** cup distilled vinegar
- **2** tablespoons washing soda
- **20** drops peppermint oil

Combine all ingredients in a spray bottle. Shake before each use. Spray directly onto the grout and wait 10 minutes. Brush clean with a small brush, then wipe away any residue with a soft, damp cloth.

Fizzy Bathroom Sink Cleaner

Kids love to watch the volcanic action that occurs when pouring vinegar over baking soda. Who knows? You might even get your kids to clean the bathroom!

- **½** cup baking soda
- **6** drops lemon or lime essential oil
- **¼** cup vinegar

Combine the baking soda and essential oil in a small cup. Sprinkle the mixture into the sink; pour the vinegar on top. After the fizz settles, scrub clean with a damp cloth or sponge. Rinse clean.

Soap Scum Remover

This formula will remove that annoying buildup that forms on soap dishes and toothbrush holders. The vinegar will produce a fizzing action.

- **1 tablespoon baking soda**
- **1 teaspoon salt**
- **2 drops essential oil of choice**
  vinegar

Combine the baking soda, salt, and essential oil in a small cup. Add just enough vinegar to make a paste. Apply to surfaces and scrub with a damp cloth or sponge. Rinse well.

Sanitizing the Toilet

One of the most important areas in the bathroom to clean, of course, is the commode. Most people think that the bowl itself is where the real nasties hide, but actually, it's relatively clean. Most germs take refuge behind and under the seat. Since this part is the one being handled most often, it needs careful and frequent sanitizing. There are some excellent bacteria busters offered here to do just that.

Germs-Be-Gone Toilet Cleaner

This antibacterial spray cleaner is especially formulated for cleaning the general surface area of the toilet, and under and behind the seat.

- 2 cups water
- ¼ cup liquid castile soap
- 1 tablespoon tea tree essential oil
- 10 drops eucalyptus or peppermint essential oil

Combine all ingredients in a spray bottle and shake well. Spray on toilet surfaces and wipe clean with a damp cloth or sponge.

No-Scrub Toilet Bowl Cleaner

Use this one in toilet bowls that have an everlasting ring around them. (Like the kind you find in the bathroom of your vacation cabin after 6 months of nonuse.) You can employ this recipe just before going to bed; by morning, even the toughest of stains will have disappeared.

- ½ cup baking soda
- ½ cup citric acid powder
- 1 cup vinegar
- 10 drops pine or lavender essential oil
- 5 drops lemon or lime essential oil

Combine all ingredients in a bowl or bottle and pour all at once into the toilet bowl. Allow to sit overnight. In the morning, just flush!

Easy-Does-It Bowl Cleaner

What could be simpler than this easy and effective formula?

- ½ cup baking soda
- ¼ cup white vinegar
- 10 drops tea tree essential oil

Combine all ingredients. Just add to the bowl, swipe with a brush, and you're done.

Natural Septic Care

If you have a well and septic system, you're likely aware of the importance of maintaining a healthy ecosystem of beneficial bacteria in your septic tank. Without it, organic material and paper cannot be broken down, which can result in a blockage of flow to your drain field or, worse, a backup of sewage into your home.

Household products, especially chlorinated products (such as bleach), can interfere with this natural process. Even if you use natural cleaning formulas exclusively in your home, there are still bound to be agents designed to kill bacteria going down the drain. Even running large amounts of plain water can weaken the bacterial status of a septic system.

The solution? Feed your septic tank some bacteria every 4 to 6 weeks. The best time to use these treatments is when the household is retiring for the night. That way, the treatment can get to work while people are less likely to use the bathroom.

Brown Sugar Bacteria Activator

The following formula may seem like a recipe for a bread starter, but it's actually medicine for your septic tank to help ensure a supply of beneficial bacteria to keep things flowing smoothly.

- **4 cups very warm water**
- **4 cups brown sugar**
- **2 packets active dry yeast**

Pour the warm water into a large bucket, then dissolve the sugar in the water. Add the yeast and stir. Set the mixture aside for 15 to 20 minutes, or until the yeast reacts with the sugar and becomes frothy. Flush this mixture down the toilet in portions — don't try to flush it all at once.

Cornmeal Bacteria Activator

This formula utilizes the starch in cornmeal in the activation process. Incidentally, if you happen to be a home brewer, these same ingredients go into making traditional moonshine!

- **4 cups very warm water**
- **2 cups cornmeal**
- **2 cups sugar**
- **2 packages active dry yeast**

Pour the warm water into a large bucket, then stir in the cornmeal. Add the sugar, stirring to dissolve. Add the yeast and stir again. Set aside until the yeast becomes activated (about 15 minutes), then flush the mixture down the toilet a little at a time.

Hand Soap & Sanitizer

As any health practitioner will tell you, frequent handwashing is key to avoid contracting contagious viruses. Believe it or not, washing with a mild, simple soap offers the most protection. The reason for this is that viruses are coated in a greasy material that protects them from detection by our immune systems. Soap neutralizes this material and allows immune system chemicals to locate and destroy them before they can invade our healthy cells. However, soap and water may not always be available. At these times, a hand sanitizer fortified with alcohol and essential oil is the next best thing.

Rosemary & Mint Hand Sanitizer

Make a double batch of this formula — one for the bath and one for the kitchen! Note: For this to be effective against viruses, be sure to use isopropyl alcohol (rubbing alcohol) in a strength of 91 percent or higher.

- ⅔ cup 91% isopropyl alcohol
- ⅓ cup pure aloe vera gel
- 10 drops rosemary essential oil
- 10 drops peppermint essential oil

Combine all ingredients in a small bowl; stir well. Transfer into a glass dispenser with a pump.

Lavender Foaming Hand Soap

This fragrant soap sanitizes while softening hands. Note: Coconut oil is solid at room temperature, unless you live in a very warm climate. A second or two in the microwave or even a rest on a sunny windowsill will liquefy it.

- ½ **cup liquid castile soap**
- ¼ **cup distilled water**
- 1 **tablespoon virgin coconut oil, melted**
- 1 **teaspoon vegetable glycerin**
- 15 **drops lavender essential oil**

Mix all ingredients together in a small bowl. Transfer into a clean pump soap dispenser.

HELPFUL HINTS FOR THE BATHROOM

To maintain a fresh scent in the bathroom, place a few drops of your favorite essential oil on the cardboard tube supporting the toilet paper. Every time the paper is used, the fragrance will be released.

Place a bowl of potpourri on the sink or toilet tank. Replace the potpourri every 3 months. For recipes, see chapter 8. Potpourri, whether made from natural or synthetic materials, can be toxic to pets and young children who might be tempted to handle or even eat it. If this scenario is a possibility in your home, you can place the potpourri on a high shelf. Or try filling a muslin or cloth bag with the pot-pourri, then hang it out of reach.

To keep bath mats and rugs smelling fresh between washings, simply scent ½ cup baking soda with 8 to 10 drops of the essential oil of your choice. Sprinkle on the carpets, wait 15 minutes, then vacuum.

If you have a stand-alone toothbrush holder, be sure to run it through the dishwasher often. You'd be amazed at the germs and dirt that thrive there. If it's really full of gunk, let it stand for 20 minutes filled with water and 2 or 3 drops of tea tree essential oil. Then wash by hand or in the dishwasher.

Don't forget to periodically clean combs and hairbrushes. Let them stand for 20 minutes in a container with 1½ cups water, ½ cup vinegar, and 20 drops of tea tree, rosemary, lavender, or eucalyptus essential oil. Rinse well and allow to air-dry before putting them away.

CHAPTER
4

THE LAUNDRY

MANUFACTURERS OF LAUNDRY PRODUCTS spend a good deal of money on advertising to convince us that their products contain "magical" ingredients that can solve every laundry problem. Well, they don't. With their cleaning power stemming from caustic bleach, EDTA, and optical brighteners (which are strong allergens), their ingredients are anything but magical. But the fact is, many commercial laundry soaps contain nearly 70 percent ordinary washing soda. The difference between them basically comes down to fragrance, color, and variations in the amount of additives.

Simple Laundry Guidelines

Before you can properly clean your dirty laundry, you need to consider what you want your washer and detergent to accomplish. It doesn't do any good to wash heavily soiled work clothes with the baby's pajamas, as oils can transfer from one to the other. Likewise, you can't expect your white shirt to easily free itself of a coffee stain if you're going to wait 3 days before washing it. So before you even lift the lid of the washer, there are some basic laundry guidelines to follow to help preserve your garments and keep them looking their best.

SORTING LAUNDRY

Your mother probably told you never to wash colored clothes with white ones. But she might not have told you that there's a lot more to sorting laundry. Here are some considerations when sorting:

The first step is to sort by color. Whites, very bright colors (such as red or orange), pastels, and dark colors should be washed separately. Next, sort heavy fabrics from delicate garments that must be laundered in the gentle cycle.

Towels, sheets, and bedspreads should be washed separately because they produce lint that will adhere to other fabrics, such as knits.

Don't forget to check the pockets of your children's jeans, jackets, and shirts! I've been surprised many times by the array of trinkets a child can collect in a pocket, including coins and partially eaten foodstuffs. On one memorable occasion, a broken ballpoint pen remained undetected until it had been through the dryer! (Although the inside of the dryer ended up with a polka-dot pattern, the ink wiped away easily with a rag moistened with vinegar and cedar essential oil.)

BEFORE YOU WASH

Pretreating is all-important if you really want to rid your clothes of stains and heavy soiling. These are the best stain-fighting tactics:

Follow this golden rule of the laundry room: Pretreat stains as soon as possible. Always rinse a stain in cold water — warm water can cause fruit and sugar stains to set in. See pages 77–80 for pretreatment formulas.

Prewash heavily soiled items to help eliminate most of the dirt without redepositing it on clothes. After running clothes through the prewash cycle, drain and wash in the regular cycle — in hot water if the fabric permits it.

Presoak old or tough stains like blood and grass for 30 minutes or more.

WATER TEMPERATURE

Your washing machine comes equipped with a water temperature control for a reason: Not all fabrics are created equal. Always follow specific instructions given on a garment's care label. To avoid damaging garments, remember:

Washing in cold water will prevent shrinkage and the release of dyes. Bright colors, lightly soiled items, and delicate garments should be washed in cold water. Rinsing in cold water is suitable for all types of laundry. And you'll be saving energy, too.

Warm water helps to reduce wrinkling and the bleeding of colors. Choose warm-water washing for permanent press, washable wool, dark colors, and synthetic fabrics.

Hot water is recommended for heavily soiled clothing, towels, whites, pastels, and light-colored prints. Never wash 100 percent cotton or 100 percent wool items in hot water or they will shrink. Instead, use cold water for cotton and hand-wash wool items.

THE DETERGENT DILEMMA

Believe it or not, you're probably using more laundry product than necessary per load. How much do you really need? The usual recommended capful is almost twice as much as required for an average load. In fact, excess detergent leads to residue that only traps dirt in the clothes you've just washed. It's not only environmentally friendly to use less, it's easier on your clothing and your budget, too.

Here are some other detergent tips:

Keep a big jug of white vinegar in your laundry area. When added to the rinse cycle, vinegar makes blankets soft and fluffy and dissolves uric acid, making it perfect for soaking or rinsing babies' items. Vinegar also reduces soap residue, breaks up grease and oil, and is a natural bleach. As an added benefit, using vinegar in the rinse cycle can help prevent static cling in the dryer.

Laundry soap doesn't perform as well in hard water, but this can be corrected by adding zeolite powder, orrisroot, or baking soda to the wash.

Wondering where to find soap flakes? Ivory Snow was the answer for decades, but the formula changed in 1991, and it became a detergent. For many years afterward, soap flakes were not commercially available, leaving only one other option: grating a bar of natural soap to use in recipes. Today, there are many companies that offer pure, unscented soap flakes to choose from online. You can still grate your own flakes — and if you are a soap maker, grating soap for these recipes is a great way to use misshapen bars you don't want to give as gifts.

The Herbal Touch

Herbal essential oils can be blended into laundry formulas (liquid or powder) or added to the softener dispenser of your machine. Essential oils not only boost cleaning power, they also provide a fresh, clean scent.

Essential oils can lend therapeutic qualities, too. For instance, add tea tree essential oil to your laundry if you suffer from frequent yeast infections. Eucalyptus essential oil can be used when someone in the household is fighting a cold. Jasmine, rose, or ylang-ylang essential oil will impart a romantic scent to fine washables. You are encouraged to experiment! You can even create your own unique blend from the essential oil chart on the next page.

Herbal-scented baking soda is another way to use essential oils in the laundry. Baking soda adds whitening power and is a natural water softener. For a 16-ounce box, use 15 to 20 drops of essential oil. You can mix it right in the box! Simply add the oils to the box and shake well.

Be creative in your thinking, and you'll soon find that you don't miss store-bought detergents at all.

Essential Oil Chart for Laundry

All of these essential oils help clean and freshen the laundry. They offer other benefits as well.

OIL	PROPERTIES
Cedar	Adds a clean, woodsy scent
Chamomile	Soothing
Eucalyptus	Excellent for colds and sinus trouble
Lavender	Relaxing
Lemon	Stimulating, helps whiten laundry
Peppermint	Good for colds and sinus trouble
Rose geranium	Adds a romantic scent
Rosemary*	Calming (but often stimulating on its own)
Sweet orange	Helps remove stains and whiten laundry
Tea tree	Antibacterial and antifungal

*Not suitable for wool, silk, or satin

Making Natural Laundry Soaps

These formulas don't have any magical components that you can't pronounce. Instead, the cleaning power of these soaps comes from combining clean, pure ingredients.

Basic Liquid Laundry Soap

This simple formula is tough on dirt but easy on your budget. This recipe makes about a quart, but you can easily double it.

  1 **tablespoon washing soda**

  1 **tablespoon baking soda**

  ¼ **cup liquid castile soap**

  20–25 **drops essential oil of choice**

  3 **cups boiling water**

  1 **cup cold water**

Combine the washing soda and baking soda in a large glass or ceramic bowl; mix well. In a small bowl, stir the castile soap and essential oil until combined. Add this to the dry ingredients; stir well. Slowly add the boiling water while gently stirring (note that the mixture will be thin). Now add the cold water, stirring gently. Using a funnel, pour the mixture into a half-gallon container. When the mixture has cooled completely, replace the cap and label the container. Use ¼ cup for an average load, ½ cup for extralarge or heavily soiled loads.

Basic Laundry Soap Powder

This easy-to-make powdered soap goes a long way!

  2 **cups finely grated castile soap**

  1 **cup washing soda**

  1 **cup baking soda blended with 20 drops essential oil of choice**

Combine all ingredients in a large container with a lid. Store in a cool, dry place. Use 2 tablespoons for an average load.

Lemon-Fresh Linen Wash

This formula can be used for any type of laundry, but it's especially nice for cotton linens that will be allowed to dry naturally in the sun after washing.

- **2 cups liquid castile soap**
- **1 cup distilled water**
- **25 drops lemon or lemongrass essential oil**

Combine all ingredients in a container with a lid. Swirl, don't shake, to mix. Use ¼ cup for an average load of linens.

Hard-Water Formula

Hard water can affect the performance of your laundry soap. This formula uses baking soda and vinegar as natural water softeners.

- **1 cup soap flakes or finely grated castile soap**
- **1 cup washing soda**
- **½ cup baking soda**
- **2 cups vinegar**
- **10 drops essential oil of choice**

Combine the soap, washing soda, and baking soda in a heavy container. Blend the vinegar and essential oil in a separate container, preferably one with a pour spout. Use ½ cup of the soap mixture for washing; add ½ cup of the vinegar mixture during the rinse cycle.

Fine Washables Formula

Rosemary is an old favorite for freshening delicate knits and lingerie. Note: Do not use on items that are silk, satin, or 100 percent wool.

- 2 **sprigs fresh rosemary or 1 teaspoon dried, or**
  - 3 **drops rosemary essential oil**
- 1 **cup boiling water**
- 1 **ounce liquid castile soap**

Bruise the fresh rosemary (slightly crush it between the fingers to release the oils), or crush the dried rosemary leaves in a bowl. Pour in the boiling water and steep for 15 minutes, then strain. Alternatively, mix the essential oil with a cup of water. Place the clothes in the washer and add the castile soap and rosemary water. Launder in cold water on the gentle cycle.

Baby's Laundry Formula

Babies can sure get their clothing messy! Baking soda and vinegar will help whiten and soften fabrics.

- 2 **drops essential oil (optional)**
- 2 **tablespoons liquid castile soap**
- ¼ **cup washing soda**
- 1¼ **cups baking soda**
- ¼ **cup white vinegar**

If using the essential oil, mix with the castile soap. Add this mixture to the washer along with the washing soda, baking soda, and vinegar. Launder as usual.

DIAPER WHITENER

Add ½ cup washing soda, ½ cup vinegar, and 6 to 8 drops of essential oil to a pail or bucket of hot water. Soak the diapers for 20 to 30 minutes, or longer if heavily soiled, before laundering.

Bright Colors Formula

This recipe makes enough for one load. You can make larger batches, but keep the liquid castile soap separate.

- 1 ounce liquid castile soap (scented with 2 to 4 drops essential oil, if desired)
- ¼ cup washing soda
- ½ cup Epsom salts

Add the liquid castile soap to the washer, then add the washing soda and Epsom salts. Launder as usual.

Lavender Laundry Bleach Alternative

Use this nontoxic solution instead of chlorinated bleach for your whites.

- 8 cups distilled water
- 2 cups hydrogen peroxide
- 1½ tablespoons citric acid powder
- 25 drops lavender essential oil

Combine all ingredients in a large container, preferably one with a pour spout. Swirl to dissolve the citric acid powder.

Add 1 cup per load to your washer's dispenser compartment for front-loading machines. Use ½ cup for high-efficiency (HE) machines.

Natural Fabrics Rescue

Natural fabrics, such as wool and silk, need special care. Wool should be hand-washed in cool water and a capful of liquid castile soap, then rinsed well in a tub of clean water. Never allow wool to soak. Nor should you attempt to wring wool dry. After the final rinse, place the wool garment on a dry towel and roll up like a jelly roll. Gently press on the towel to remove excess water. Repeat this process if necessary with another towel. Then place the garment flat on a dry towel, reshape, and leave it to dry.

Silk items should be dipped in a solution of warm water and a capful of liquid castile soap. Rinse well and gently squeeze out excess water. Turn the garment inside out and hang until it is just damp to the touch. With the garment still reversed, press with an iron on low setting.

PRETREATMENTS FOR STAINS

Since vinegar can remove some dyes, test these formulas on a small, hidden area of the fabric before treating the actual stain.

Tea Tree & Salt Presoak

This stain remover is another great vinegar–based solution.

> 1 **cup vinegar**
> ½ **cup salt**
> 3 **drops tea tree essential oil**

Place the clothes in the washer and add enough warm water to cover them. Combine all ingredients and add to the washer. Let the clothes soak for an hour or longer, then wash as usual.

Perspiration Stain Remover

Use this formula to pretreat ring around the collar and perspiration stains.

> ¼ **cup vinegar**
> 4 **drops lemon, lime, or eucalyptus essential oil**
> 1 **tablespoon baking soda**

Combine all ingredients. Rub the mixture into the stains with your fingers, a soft cloth, or an old toothbrush. Launder as usual.

Lemon & Tea Tree Perspiration Presoak

Try this fresh-smelling pretreatment before you wash.

- 1 **cup vinegar**
- ¼ **cup lemon juice**
- 6 **drops tea tree essential oil**

Combine all ingredients and add to the clothes in a washer full of warm water. Allow to soak for an hour or two, then wash as usual.

All-Purpose Stain Spray

Since food and drink spills aren't likely to occur while you're in the laundry room, why not make up extra bottles and keep this formula handy in the kitchen and bath as well?

- ¼ **cup vegetable oil–based soap**
- ¼ **cup glycerin**
- 2 **tablespoons washing soda**
- 10 **drops peppermint or tea tree essential oil**
- 1¾ **cups water**

Combine all ingredients in a spray bottle and shake well. Spray generously onto stains. Launder as usual.

On-the-Spot Stain Lifter

Accidents happen, but this stain remover will make you forget the stain was ever there.

- **2 tablespoons cream of tartar**
- **2 drops peppermint, eucalyptus, or lemon essential oil**
- **water**

Combine all ingredients in a small cup, using just enough water to make a paste. Spread the paste over the stain and allow it to dry completely before washing.

Tricks for Wool & Silk

Sometimes, a small stain is all that stands between your wearing a wool jacket or silk blouse again and wearing it out completely with repeated cleanings. This simple spot treatment can help remove unsightly stains without cleaning the entire garment. This treatment can be used on most fabrics (including wool or silk), but don't try this on rayon.

The method: Moisten a cotton ball with white vinegar, being careful to avoid saturation. Gently dab the cotton ball onto the stain, but don't rub. Let the vinegar work for a minute or two. Then blot the stain with a dry, clean cloth several times.

BABY YOUR SILK

Since silk is a protein fiber, it cannot withstand coming into contact with soap that has a pH of 10 or higher. Like human hair, silk fibers have a natural coating of oils that must be preserved to stay looking good. In fact, this coating helps the material resist dirt and stains. Gentle hand-washing is the best way to avoid risking damage to silk from high alkali agents and the agitator of the washing machine.

Combine a capful of low pH castile soap (such as Dr. Bronner's Baby Unscented Pure-Castile Liquid Soap) in a small tub or basin full of cool or lukewarm water, swirling with your hand to distribute the soap. Place the silk garment into the water and gently dip it up and down several times (you mustn't allow silk to soak). Rinse thoroughly in cool or lukewarm water (never hot!), but don't wring or twist the garment. Lay the garment flat on some towels and, using your hands, press the excess water out. Then let the item hang dry.

REVIVE FADED OR YELLOWED SILK

Hand-wash as described above, but add one of the following to the wash water: ¼ cup hydrogen peroxide, ¼ cup white vinegar, or 15 drops of tea tree oil diluted in ¼ cup cool water. Follow the directions above for rinsing and drying the silk garment.

BE COOL WITH WOOL

You can hand-wash wool items in the same manner as described for silk garments, except you should gently squeeze the wool garment while washing, don't dip. Also, do not hang wool to dry. Instead, it must be allowed to dry on a flat surface.

Laundry Problem-Solvers

Sometimes, real life happens, and we can't always tend to a stain right away. Or the stain is the worst you can ask for, such as red wine, blood, or ink. But before you toss the garment out or make it into a dust cloth, give one of these natural remedies a try. If a stain doesn't come out the first time, it's worth repeating the process. Whatever you do, don't put the garment into the dryer if the stain is still visible after air-drying; doing so could make the stain permanent.

The following is a list of the most troublesome types of stains and some suggested remedies. Some of these stain problem-solvers involve herbal teas or extracts, while others call for other easy-to-use natural ingredients that you probably have on hand.

Baby formula. Soy-based formulas in particular can leave an ugly stain. But if formula stains are treated when they land on clothing, they can sometimes leave a ring after laundering.

Treat either type of stain by rubbing it with a mixture of vinegar and a few drops of garlic juice. This will help break down the protein in the formula and release it from the fabric. A little moistened meat tenderizer will do the same thing. I also discovered long ago that baby wipes — which are basically a combination of alcohol, mild cleanser, and emollients — will remove these stains beautifully if applied right away, and are safe for most fabrics. Choose the method that's best for the age of the stain and the type of fabric that you're treating.

Berries. If the stain is fresh, rub a slice of lemon over it several times. If the stain is old, treat it with glycerin and wait 30 minutes. Rinse and allow to air-dry. If the stain endures, make a mixture of 1 heaping tablespoon cornstarch, 2 drops of eucalyptus essential oil, and 1 teaspoon glycerin. Add just enough water to make a thick paste and spread on the stain. Without rinsing, put the garment in the sun to dry. Repeat the paste application if necessary. Once the stain is gone, you can launder as usual.

Blood. Immediately rinse the garment thoroughly in cool water. If necessary, let the garment soak in a solution of laundry soap and water for several hours. For light-colored fabrics, try wiping with a soft cloth moistened with hydrogen peroxide. Hang the garment in the sun and keep applying hydrogen peroxide until all traces of the stain are gone. Allow to dry and launder as usual.

Butter or margarine. Make a paste of 1 tablespoon baking soda; 2 drops of lemon, lime, or orange essential oil; and water. Spread the paste on the stain and allow to dry, then wash as usual.

Candle wax. First harden the wax with ice cubes and gently peel off as much as you can. Then place the stained area between paper towels and press with a warm iron. Keep moving or replacing the paper towels to avoid transferring the candle wax back into the fabric. Continue this procedure until the paper towels no longer absorb the wax. The remaining stain should then be treated with a little glycerin on a cotton ball and laundered as usual.

Chewing gum. If chewing gum makes its way onto clothing, put the garment in a bag and place in the freezer for 30 to 45 minutes. The gum should pull right off. If a residue remains, soak in full-strength vinegar before washing.

Chocolate. Make a paste of washing soda and water and spread over the stain. Allow to dry, and then launder as usual.

Coffee and tea. Immediately flush with cool water. Then soak in a washing soda and water solution before laundering.

Egg. Scrape off any dried material. Douse the remaining stain with a mixture of 2 teaspoons lemon juice and 3 drops of sweet orange or lemon essential oil. Wash in cold water.

Grass. Soak the garment in vinegar, then spread a paste of baking soda and water over the stain. Wash in hot water.

Grease. Cover the stain with a mixture of 2 teaspoons each of cornmeal, salt, and baking soda. Let this mixture stand for 30 minutes or more to absorb as much grease as possible, then wipe away. Soak the remaining stain in ½ cup vinegar, 5 drops of lemon or orange essential oil or grapefruit seed extract, and ¼ cup water until the stain breaks free. If the fabric can tolerate it, wash in hot water.

Ink. Place a cloth under the fabric and dab the stain repeatedly with undiluted eucalyptus essential oil until it begins to break up. The ink will begin to transfer to the underlying cloth. Remove as much of the stain as you can with this method. Then soak the garment in a solution of equal parts vinegar and milk before washing.

Linens. Linens can sometimes yellow if stored in a trunk or closet for a long time. The best prevention is to wrap them carefully in acid-free paper before storing. If yellowing does occur, you can soak them in a tea made from two or three fresh rhubarb stalks and 3 cups boiling water. Allow the material to dry in the sun. Repeat as necessary until the stains have disappeared. You can also use 1 cup lemon juice diluted in 2 cups water in place of the rhubarb tea.

Lipstick. Gently massage the stain with white toothpaste or 3 or 4 drops of glycerin for a few minutes, blot dry, then wipe several times with eucalyptus essential oil. Launder as usual. Repeat the eucalyptus application if the stain doesn't come out completely after washing.

Mold and mildew. Sometimes towels are left in a duffel bag after a day at the beach, or clothes are put into storage while still damp, resulting in mold or mildew stains. Pretreat these stains with a solution of ¼ cup vinegar, 1 teaspoon salt, and 6 drops of tea tree essential oil. Launder as usual.

Mustard. Mustard contains turmeric, which yields a bright yellow dye. To break up the stain, apply some glycerin and let stand for 30 minutes. Then gently massage some laundry soap (liquid or powder) into the stain and wash as usual.

Nail polish. First try blotting the stain with rubbing alcohol. If this doesn't work, test some nail polish remover in an inconspicuous place on the garment. If the test area of the fabric isn't damaged, proceed to the stain. *Note:* Organic nail polish removers are available at health food stores that carry natural cosmetics.

Oil. Carefully blot up excess oil from the garment, then follow the treatment recommended for grease stains on page 85.

Paint. Success depends on the type of paint involved. Latex paint is easily removed by rinsing in hot, soapy water. Oil-based paint is another matter, and your best chance is to act immediately. Rub the stain with rubbing alcohol, then soak in a solution of equal parts hot vinegar and milk for several hours. If this doesn't work, you may have to take the garment to a professional cleaner or accept the fact that it's now a dust cloth.

Pencil. Pencil marks may seem innocent, but they can persist after washing. The cure is simple: Rub them off with an eraser before washing.

Rust. Make a paste of lemon juice and salt. Let the paste sit on the stain for several minutes, then pour boiling water over the stain. Or boil the garment in 1 tablespoon cream of tartar and 1 quart water. An old-fashioned but time-tested remedy for rust stains is to let the fabric soak in a cooled infusion made from two or three fresh rhubarb stalks and 3 cups boiling water.

Salad dressing. Soak the garment in a solution of ½ cup vinegar, ½ cup lemon juice, and 6 to 8 drops of sweet orange, eucalyptus, or tea tree essential oil for 30 minutes. Then launder as usual, in hot water if the fabric permits it.

Scorch marks. For light-colored fabrics, test a small area with hydrogen peroxide. If no damage occurs, treat the stain by dabbing on hydrogen peroxide, then hang the garment in direct sunlight. Keep the stain moistened with additional hydrogen peroxide until the scorch marks fade. For darker clothing, coat the stain with glycerin and allow to rest overnight. Then wash as usual. If any residue from the glycerin remains after washing, it can be removed by rubbing with liquid castile soap and rinsing thoroughly.

Shoe polish. Water or any other wet treatment will cause this stain to spread. Instead, blot the stain with glycerin on a soft, clean cloth to loosen it from the garment's fibers, then launder as usual.

Tar. Fresh tar can be countered by first scraping off surface pieces with a warm butter knife. Dried tar should first be treated with glycerin or olive oil to soften it. Then place the garment over several folded paper towels and pour on 2 or 3 drops of eucalyptus essential oil. The paper towels will absorb the dissolving tar underneath, so replace them as needed. Keep working with the knife during this process to scrape off the lifting tar. Repeat this process until the tar has been removed.

Urine. Soak the material in a solution of 1 cup vinegar, 5 drops of lavender essential oil, and, if the fabric can tolerate it, 1 cup very hot water for 30 minutes. Then wash as usual.

Wine. Rinse in cool water right away, then follow the procedure on page 83 for removing berry stains.

Fabric Softeners

Vinegar is the fabric softener of choice for many reasons. Not only is it nontoxic, it also removes soap residue in the rinse cycle and helps prevent static cling in the dryer. The fun part lies in using different scented vinegars. Essential oils can produce a fresh, clean, floral, woodsy, or spicy effect — use whatever fragrance suits your fancy.

Adding 1 or 2 cups of vinegar to the rinse cycle is fine for whites, but more than that can cause some dyes to run, especially from rayon fabrics. Keep the color and fabric in mind when using these formulas.

Lavender Fabric Softener

Formulas don't get much easier than this one, which is both fragrant and effective.

> **20** drops lavender essential oil
>
> **1** gallon vinegar

Add the lavender essential oil to the vinegar right in the container and you've got instant fabric softener! Shake well before using. For a large load, add 1 cup during the rinse cycle; use ½ cup during the rinse cycle for smaller loads.

Orange Glow Fabric Softener

White vinegar softens hard water and reduces static cling. The addition of sweet orange essential oil provides a fresh, clean scent.

- **8 cups water**
- **6 cups white vinegar**
- **1 cup baking soda**
- **25 drops sweet orange essential oil**

Combine all ingredients in a large jug. Shake well before adding ½ cup to the rinse cycle.

Minty-Fresh Fabric Softener

This formula helps remove tough odors from clothing.

- **1 gallon vinegar**
- **10 drops peppermint essential oil**

Combine the vinegar and essential oil in a heavy-duty container. Add 1 cup to the rinse cycle for each load.

Lemony Fabric Softener

There's nothing like the smell of lemons to suggest freshness.

- **6 cups vinegar**
- **1 cup water**
- **1 cup baking soda**
- **15 drops lemon or lemongrass essential oil**

Combine all ingredients in a heavy-duty container. Add 1 cup to the rinse cycle for each load for truly lemon-fresh clothes.

Fabric Softener Crystals

Use this formula if you have hard water with a high mineral content. In addition to adding a pleasant scent to laundered clothing, it will help reduce static cling in the dryer.

3 cups Epsom salts

25 drops lavender essential oil

10 drops sweet orange essential oil

Combine all ingredients in a small bowl. Transfer to a jar or other container with a lid. To use, add 1 or 2 tablespoons at the same time you add detergent and wash the laundry as usual. Store in a cool, dry location.

Citrus "Oxy" Treatment

Tough stains call for tough measures. Hydrogen peroxide is an alternative to bleach, while washing soda and orange essential oil team up against odors and grease.

½ cup distilled water

½ cup hydrogen peroxide

2 tablespoons washing soda

15 drops sweet orange essential oil

Combine all ingredients in a spray bottle; shake well. To use, spray directly onto stains. Allow the treatment to work for 30 to 60 minutes before laundering the item.

DRYER SHEETS

This idea is clever and simple — natural dryer sheets can be made from a scrap of cotton cloth and 3 to 5 drops of your favorite essential oil. Using more may actually soil your newly washed laundry. Here are some interesting combinations you could try:

* Cedar and patchouli for a masculine, woodsy scent
* Rosemary and thyme for an earthy scent
* Geranium and neroli (orange blossom) for a floral scent
* Peppermint and eucalyptus for cold sufferers
* Jasmine and ylang-ylang for a romantic scent
* Sweet orange and lemon for a refreshing scent
* Chamomile and hyssop for a relaxing effect (helps insomnia!)

Cut a scrap of cotton cloth into a small square (about 4 inches), and add 3 to 5 drops of your favorite essential oil. Toss into the dryer with the rest of the laundry. You can use the same cloth two or three times, each time refreshing it with 3 more drops of essential oil. After that, wash the cloth and it's ready to be used again.

Natural Moth Repellents

When it comes time to store your wool sweaters and coats, you'll want to keep moths away so you'll find your garments in one piece the following season. Aside from the terrible smell that regular mothballs give off (which seeps into clothing), they contain paradichlorobenzene, which is very toxic. The following alternatives are safe and just as effective.

Tuck away sachets of cedar chips with your wool items.

If storing your items in a trunk or other container, place a tea towel or a sheet of tissue paper that has been sprinkled with several drops of lavender and rosemary essential oils on top.

If your clothing will be hanging, also hang a few whole, dried lemon peels in the closet where the clothing will be stored.

Lavender Linen Drawer Liners

Keeping lingerie and clothing fresh couldn't be easier with this fragrant idea. When the lavender flowers have lost their scent, simply open the fabric pocket and replace the flower buds with fresh ones.

cotton or linen fabric, to line drawers

Velcro strips (the kind with the sticky backing)

1 cup dried lavender flowers

1. Measure the bottom of the drawer you wish to line and cut two pieces of fabric to fit snugly inside. Press the Velcro strips around the edge of each piece of fabric so that the pieces will hook to each other when pressed together.

2. Spread the dried lavender flowers in an even layer on one piece of the fabric with the Velcro facing up. Place the other precut fabric on top, Velcro facing down. Press down on the fabric edges to secure the Velcro and seal the lavender inside.

Geranium Gift-Wrap Closet Liners

Make use of leftover gift wrap and keep towels and linens smelling sweet at the same time. You can also use this lining in bathroom drawers or in kitchen cupboards and pantries.

> **gift wrap**
> **5–6 drops geranium essential oil**

Measure the shelf or drawer that you'll be lining so you can cut the gift wrap to the right size. After cutting, smooth out the gift wrap on a table, printed-side down. Moisten a cotton ball with the essential oil and rub it lengthwise across the paper. Line the closet shelf (or drawer) with the scented gift wrap, scented side down. *Note:* To keep the lining from slipping, use a staple gun to secure the corner edges to the shelf. This makes removal of the liner much easier than using tape or glue.

Laundry Starch

Here's a quick alternative to the commercial, chemical–laden starches. For light colors, leave out the black tea and increase water by ½ cup.

> 1 cup water
>
> 2 tablespoons cornstarch
>
> 2 drops essential oil of choice (for light colors, use a clear oil like tea tree)
>
> ½ cup cooled black tea (for dark colors only)

Combine all ingredients in a spray bottle. Shake well before each use. Lightly spray the garment and iron as usual.

WOOD CARE

IT ISN'T NECESSARY TO USE AN OILY PRODUCT every time you dust your furniture. In fact, some types of furniture never need oil, just a dusting with a damp cloth. Some older pieces and unfinished wood, however, can benefit from an occasional oil treatment.

It's the same story with hardwood flooring — some floors are given a surface finish and others a penetrating finish. If your hardwood floor has a shiny, glossy appearance, it probably has a coating of varnish, such as polyurethane. For this type of flooring, regular cleaning with a vegetable-oil wood soap will remove any surface dirt and restore a high sheen. If your floor doesn't come back to life after cleaning, it may need a new surface finish. If your floor has a slightly oily feel when you draw your hand across it, it likely has a penetrating finish and needs additional waxing now and then to protect it.

Wood Cleaners

These formulas are for furniture with a hard finish and in need of a good surface cleaning, like garage and estate-sale finds, or items kept in storage for a long time. If cleaning the wood doesn't revive the piece, it may be time for refinishing.

Fragrant Wood Cleaner

This fragrant formula will clear away sticky grime. Using bergamot or geranium essential oil will give a floral scent.

½ cup lemon juice

1 teaspoon liquid castile soap

4 drops bergamot, geranium, or sweet orange essential oil

Combine all ingredients in a small spray bottle. Apply to the wood and wipe clean with a damp cloth. Wipe again with a dry cloth.

BE WOOD WARY

Always test wood-cleaning formulas on an inconspicuous area of your furniture, like the inside of a leg or a panel underneath, before treating the entire piece. This step is a very important one, as some essential oils can adversely affect certain wood finishes.

Dusting Aids

These formulas are useful for regular dusting, and they smell great, too. Choose one that's right for the type of wood you have.

Lemon-Fresh Dust Buster

This recipe is for a single use. You could make larger quantities, but the presence of lemon juice necessitates refrigeration. If you want to make enough to store in a spray bottle, you could increase the amount of lemon balm tea to 2 cups, omit the lemon juice, and increase the lemon essential oil to 20 drops.

¼ cup lemon juice

⅛ cup cooled lemon balm tea

2 drops thyme essential oil

4 drops lemon essential oil

Combine all ingredients in a spray bottle and shake well. Spray onto the wood and wipe clean with a dry cloth.

Cedarwood Dusting Aid

Here's my personal favorite! I use it for bookcases, coffee tables, kitchen cabinets, and the antique dining room table that we refinished a few years back. I adore the scent of cedar on wood; the sweet orange oil adds just the right touch. This recipe makes enough for a large spray bottle.

- ½ cup oil soap (I like Murphy's Oil Soap)
- ¾ cup water
- 5 drops sweet orange essential oil
- 15–20 drops cedar essential oil

Combine all ingredients in a spray bottle and shake well. Spray onto the wood and wipe clean with a soft, dry cloth.

Moisture-Rich Duster

This recipe is nourishing for older, dry wood. But use it sparingly, as too much oil left on the wood will attract more dust. Adjust the amount of flaxseed and essential oils needed based on how much surface area you are treating.

- scant ⅛ cup flaxseed oil
- 3 drops lemon or sweet orange essential oil

Combine the oils in a small cup and stir to mix. Apply small amounts at a time to a dry cloth and rub well into the wood. Wipe with a dry cloth to remove any oil residue.

Wood Polishes, Washes & Waxes

You can make larger batches of any of these formulas and store them in a recycled coffee can or glass jar with a screw-top lid. Just be sure to shake or stir before applying to the polishing cloth. Keeping an old toothbrush or small paintbrush in the can or jar is an easy and less messy way of getting the liquid polish onto the cloth.

Herbal Wood Polish

This formula leaves a light herbal aroma.

> ¼ cup flaxseed oil
>
> 3 drops lavender or rosemary essential oil

Combine the oils in a bowl. Apply a light layer of polish to the wood with a brush or cloth. Rub into the wood with a soft cloth, using circular motions. Wipe again with a dry cloth.

Lemon-Walnut Wood Polish

If making a larger quantity to store, use 15 drops of lemon essential oil instead of the lemon juice.

> ¼ cup lemon juice
>
> ⅛ cup walnut oil
>
> ⅛ cup flaxseed oil

Combine all ingredients in a bowl (or clean coffee can with lid, if making in quantity). Apply a light layer of polish to the wood with a brush or cloth. Rub into the wood with a soft cloth, using circular motions. Wipe again with a dry cloth.

Carnauba & Lavender Wood Paste

Carnauba is the hardest wax available. Combined with oil, it is an excellent wood restorative.

2 tablespoons carnauba wax flakes
1 cup flaxseed, almond, walnut, or olive oil
6 drops lavender essential oil

1. Combine the carnauba and flaxseed oil in the top of a double boiler. Heat slowly, stirring until completely melted.
2. Remove from the heat, add the essential oil, and blend well. Pour into a glass or tin container and allow to cool completely before sealing.
3. To use, spread the paste on the wood with a soft, dry cloth using small, circular motions. Buff with a second dry cloth.

FURNITURE FIX

If grease is spilled or splattered on wooden furniture, immediately cover the stain with salt to absorb as much grease as possible. Wait an hour, then vacuum or carefully brush away the salt with a dry cloth.

If a grease stain remains, put a soft towel over the spot and press with a warm iron — but be careful not to scorch the wood! Keep shifting the towel around, or replace it with a fresh one, to avoid redepositing grease on the wood.

Traditional Beeswax Polish

This formula is used on quality wood pieces (especially antique furniture) that have been treated with a light penetrating finish; do not use on lacquered, painted, or unfinished surfaces. The formula calls for turpentine, but you can substitute a citrus peel–derived product called Citrus Solvent, made by The Real Milk Paint Company. If using turpentine, take extra care in handling and storing.

  8 ounces unrefined beeswax, grated
2½ cups turpentine
  2 cups water
  ½ cup lemon juice
  2 ounces grated castile soap
 15 drops essential oil of choice

1. Melt the beeswax slowly in the top of a double boiler. When melted, remove from the heat and carefully stir in the turpentine. Set aside.
2. Bring the water and lemon juice to a boil in a medium saucepan. Add the castile soap and stir until the soap melts. Allow this mixture to cool for 5 minutes.
3. Very slowly, pour the lemon juice mixture in a fine stream into the beeswax mixture, stirring constantly. Add the essential oil and blend well. Pour into a shallow glass jar or tin can and let cool completely before putting the lid on.
4. Dip a soft, dry cloth into the polish and spread a small amount on the wood surface; use small, circular motions. Wipe and buff with a second dry cloth.

Hardwood Floor Wash

If you have loose boards or wood tiles, hand-wipe these areas with the wash. Excess liquid from the mop can get in the cracks and cause further buckling.

1½ cups water

1½ cups vinegar

20 drops peppermint essential oil

Combine all ingredients in a spray bottle. Use sparingly, working on small sections of the floor. Dry mop the floor after washing.

Double-Nut Wood Polish

This one smells almost good enough to eat! (But don't.)

¼ cup almond oil

⅛ cup walnut oil

4 drops pure vanilla extract

Combine all ingredients in a bowl. Apply a light layer of polish to the wood with a brush or cloth. Rub into the wood with a soft cloth, using circular motions. Wipe again with a dry cloth.

WOOD PANELING

Most wood paneling can be damaged by liquids and only requires occasional dusting with a soft cloth. If it has an oily finish, however, you can mist the cloth with Cedar-wood Dusting Aid or an oily cleaner such as Moisture-Rich Duster (see page 100 for both recipes). Test the formula on a small area first.

Citrus-Scented Wood Floor Wax

In this formula, the lemon juice and essential oils clean while the beeswax and carnauba wax nourish.

1 cup flaxseed oil

¼ cup lemon juice, plus more for rubbing

2 tablespoons grated beeswax

2 tablespoons carnauba wax flakes

6 drops lemon essential oil

2 drops sweet orange essential oil

1. Place the flaxseed oil, lemon juice, and waxes in the top of a double boiler over low heat. Stir constantly until completely melted and smooth.

2. Add the essential oils. Remove from the heat and pour the mixture into a clean coffee can and allow to harden.

3. Once the wax has hardened, tap the sides of the can until the wax breaks free. Turn out the wax and gently rub it on the floor, like a crayon. Saturate a cloth with lemon juice, wring it out, and rub the wax tracings well into the floor. Buff with a clean, dry cloth.

Woodsy Wood Floor Wax

This formula leaves behind a nice shine and an earthy scent.

   2 **cups flaxseed oil**
  ¼ **cup lemon juice, plus more for rubbing**
  ¼ **cup carnauba wax flakes**
   2 **tablespoons beeswax**
   8 **drops patchouli essential oil**
  10 **drops cedar essential oil**

1. Combine the flaxseed oil, lemon juice, and waxes in the top of a double boiler over low heat. Stir constantly until all the wax is melted.

2. Add the essential oils and blend well. Remove from the heat. Pour into a clean coffee can and allow to harden.

3. Once the wax has hardened, tap the sides of the can until the wax breaks free. Turn out the wax and gently rub it on the floor, like a crayon. Saturate a cloth with lemon juice, wring it out, and rub the wax tracings well into the floor. Buff with a clean, dry cloth.

Wax Remover

This formula is for wood floors without a protective varnish finish.

- 2 **cups warm vinegar**
- ½ **cup lemon juice**
- ½ **cup water**
- 1 **capful liquid castile soap**
- 10 **drops essential oil of choice**

Combine all ingredients in a bucket. Dampen a sponge mop or soft-bristled brush with the formula and apply to the floor in sections, using short strokes. Wipe each floor section dry with a towel or clean mop before moving on to the next.

SOLUTIONS FOR WOOD PROBLEMS

Black heel marks. These can be removed by rubbing 2 or 3 drops of cedar or eucalyptus essential oil over the mark with a soft cloth.

Burns. For burns that have not penetrated the wood surface but have just left a mark, rub with a thin paste of rottenstone (or cigarette ashes), flaxseed oil, and 2 or 3 drops of peppermint or tea tree essential oil. (*Note:* Tea tree oil is not recommended for dark wood.) If the burn has penetrated the wood surface, you may have to refinish the area.

Crayon. Wipe crayon marks with a few drops of cedar, peppermint, or tea tree essential oil mixed with a dab of toothpaste. (*Note:* Tea tree oil is not recommended for dark wood.) Wipe clean with a cloth moistened with vinegar.

Grease on floors. Immediately place ice cubes on top of the spill to harden and prevent the grease from seeping further into the wood. If a grease layer forms, it can be scraped off with a blunt object, such as a popsicle stick. If the wood is unfinished or has a penetrating finish, squirt some vegetable oil soap and a few drops of eucalyptus essential oil over the spill. Blot the stain repeatedly with clean paper towels or cotton cloths.

Painted wood floors. Wood floors that have been painted can be cleaned with a solution of 2 teaspoons washing soda and 1 cup rosemary or sage tea (strained and cooled) mixed with a gallon of warm water.

Scratches. For light-colored woods, wet a soft cloth with equal parts lemon juice and olive or vegetable oil and gently rub into the wood. Scratches on walnut can be treated with — what else? — a freshly shelled raw walnut. Darker woods, like mahogany, can be treated with a cloth dipped in equal amounts of warm water and vinegar. If the scratch remains, you can fill it in with a crayon or oil pastel pencil. Scratch marks on wood floors may be removed by gently rubbing in a circular motion with very fine steel wool moistened with a hard wax, such as Citrus-Scented Wood Floor Wax (page 105) or Woodsy Wood Floor Wax (page 106).

Water stains and rings. Leaking vases and flowerpots or condensation from cold drink glasses can leave bleached rings on wood surfaces. To treat these stains, first remove old polish by wiping with a soft cloth dipped in full-strength vinegar. Wipe thoroughly with a dry cloth. Then apply mayonnaise or flaxseed oil, working from the outside to the center of the spot. Leave the oil or mayonnaise for several hours, then buff with a cloth. You can also rub 2 to 4 drops of peppermint essential oil on the stain. Toothpaste is reputedly another cure for water rings on wood. Whatever method you use, remember to test on an inconspicuous spot first.

CHAPTER

6

CLEANING METALS

METAL POLISHES MAY CONTAIN ONE OR MORE strong acids that quickly dissolve tarnish. These acids can also burn human skin. Hydrofluoric acid, used in some rust removers and aluminum polishes, is probably the most hazardous. If it gets on your skin, it continues to penetrate until it permeates the bone. Of course, protective gloves should be worn when handling such chemicals, but in spite of any precautions taken, does this sound like something you want to put your hands in? Worse yet, do you want to apply it to utensils and vessels that are used to serve food?

Removing Metal Stains & Buildup

Many people are convinced that a caustic commercial polish is necessary to adequately perform the task of removing rust and tarnish from metals. But you probably already have the ingredients readily available in your kitchen or garden to do the job safely and to do it well. You may not have the instant results that might be achieved with a commercial polish, but you will get good results if you allow some time for the formulas suggested here to work. Besides, rust and tarnish do not develop overnight — why expect them to disappear in a moment?

ALUMINUM

Aluminum is the most abundant metal found in the earth's crust and is usually found as aluminum silicate or mixed with other minerals such as iron, calcium, and magnesium. Since the expense of extracting the aluminum from these silicate mixtures is too great, bauxite, an impure hydrated oxide, is the common source of commercial aluminum.

When in contact with air, new aluminum quickly forms a durable oxide layer that protects it from corrosion. This layer is why aluminum products never rust or tarnish. Aluminum is, however, highly reactive, and two commonly used ingredients in homemade metal cleaners should never be used on it: baking soda and washing soda.

Since aluminum resists corrosion and tarnish, superficial stains are the only problems to contend with. Spruce up your aluminum by cleaning with one of these methods:

Vinegar-citrus solution. In a sink or a tub, mix 2 cups boiling water, 1 cup vinegar, and 1 teaspoon of any citrus essential oil. Place items in the solution and let soak for an hour or more. Rinse and dry well before storing.

Cornstarch-citrus paste. Combine 2 tablespoons cornstarch, 2 tablespoons alum, 5 drops of lemon or orange essential oil, and enough water to make a thick paste. While wearing gloves, rub the paste onto the metal until clean. Rinse and dry well.

Cream of tartar–citrus paste. Make a paste of ¼ cup vinegar and 2 tablespoons cream of tartar; add 2 to 4 drops of a citrus essential oil, if desired. Spread the paste on the metal and rub with your glove-protected fingers until it is clean. Rinse and dry well.

Rhubarb (or tomato) soak. For utensils, place 1 cup sliced rhubarb in 2 cups water (or enough water to submerge the items in a pot). Simmer for 30 minutes. Rinse the utensils in cool water and dry. Fresh or canned tomato slices can be used in place of the rhubarb.

BRASS

Brass is an alloy of copper and zinc. Most brass items acquired in recent years will have a lacquer finish to retard tarnish. You can maintain the shine of these items with a weekly dusting and an occasional bath in warm, sudsy water. Never use hot water to clean brass items or the lacquer finish may begin to peel away from the metal. After cleaning, you can polish the brass to a shine with a bit of olive oil, which will help the metal resist tarnish.

Older pieces of brass will oxidize over time and become tarnished, developing a greenish tinge. Here are a few ways to restore brass to its original beauty:

Citrus-salt paste. Dissolve 4 drops of any citrus essential oil and 2 teaspoons salt in 1 cup vinegar. Add just enough all-purpose flour to make a thick paste. Smear the paste onto the brass and rub with a dry sponge. Let the paste completely dry, then rinse in warm water. Dry and polish to a shine.

Citrus-vinegar polish. Combine ¼ cup vinegar, ¼ cup Worcestershire sauce, 3 drops of lemon essential oil, and 3 drops of grapefruit seed extract. Using a soft sponge, apply this solution to the metal and rub well. If the item is very tarnished, let it soak for 30 minutes or more in this solution. Then rinse and dry thoroughly.

Milk bath. Soak your brass pieces in 1 cup warm water and 1 cup milk (or more for larger pieces — just use equal parts milk and water). Milk contains lactic acid, a natural solvent.

Lemon–cream of tartar paste. Make a paste of ¼ cup lemon juice, 4 to 6 drops of orange or lemon essential oil, and 2 to 3 tablespoons cream of tartar. Rub the paste on with your fingers (wear protective gloves) using small circular motions. Let the paste dry. Then rinse and dry with a cloth.

SPECIAL CASES

You need to be careful when cleaning antique brass items so that you don't disturb the aged coloring of the piece, or what is referred to as its patina.

The best way to clean most pieces is to start with a bath in warm, soapy water to remove filmy dirt and grease. Then polish with a soft cloth moistened in flaxseed oil. Brass andirons should be cleaned with extra-fine steel wool, rubbing the metal in one direction only.

If you have a very old or delicate piece and are not sure how to approach cleaning it, you may want to consult with an expert, such as an antiques dealer, refinisher, or museum curator.

BRONZE

Bronze is also an alloy of copper, but unlike brass, it is combined with almost any other metal but zinc. Like brass, however, solid bronze pieces are often lacquered to prevent tarnishing. Good-quality bronze pieces, especially those displayed outdoors, develop a lovely patina as they age. Since this weathered effect is highly desirable in bronze, regular dusting and light polishing with a soft cloth are generally all you need to do. A soft brush can be used on items that have been neglected for a time. If you want a high polish on a bronze item, wipe it clean, then shine it with a cloth dipped in a liquid wax.

Bronze is susceptible to bronze disease, characterized by isolated spots of corrosion and light green patches. This spotting is caused by exposure to chlorides, sulfides, or excessive moisture. Usually, this disease can be remedied by bathing the piece in boiled distilled water, changing the water several times during the process. It may be necessary to soak the item for several days. You can also use hot vinegar and salt, or even hot buttermilk. If these treatments don't cure the problem, you'll need to call an expert.

To clean dirt and grease from bronze, pull on protective gloves and rub the item vigorously with a cloth moistened with a solution of 1 cup vinegar, ⅛ cup grapefruit juice, and 6 drops of pine or cedar essential oil. Rinse in warm water and dry completely with a soft, clean towel.

CAST IRON

My father is a native of Alabama, where cornbread is a staple and often made in a cast-iron skillet. My family had such a skillet, and one day I decided to give the pan a good scrubbing with soap and water and left it to air-dry in the dish rack. When I returned to put the pan away, I puzzled over how it became dirty looking again. In fact, it looked worse than before! My mistake, of course, was in letting the pan air-dry and form rust.

Cast iron will oxidize and rust if not kept completely dry at all times. It must also be seasoned with oil to form a protective barrier and prevent oxidation. When you acquire a new piece of cast iron, you need to clean it with a mild soap and fine steel wool and dry it by hand immediately. Then the interior should be wiped with a bit of vegetable oil and the pan set in a low-temperature oven (250°F/120°C) for 2 hours. After the pan has cooled, wipe it out and wash once more, taking care to dry it thoroughly. Now the pan is properly seasoned and ready to use.

After each use, cast iron should be wiped and quickly washed and dried. Another application of oil is needed before storing the pan. Cast-iron pans should not be stored with the lids in place, as this can trap moisture. It's also a good idea to place a paper towel inside the pan when storing to absorb excess moisture. If it becomes necessary to scour cast iron to remove cooked-on foods, it will be necessary to reseason the pan.

CHROME

Chrome is a hard metal with a whitish-blue appearance. Its durability and shine make it suitable for plating other metals to extend the life of the object. Chrome, or chromium, is frequently found on appliances such as toasters, ovens, refrigerators, faucets, vehicles — even golf clubs. If kept free of grease and sticky grime, chrome can last a very long time. *Note:* Never use an abrasive cleaner on chrome that may scratch or pit the surface.

To safely clean chrome, apply club soda or vinegar with a soft cloth. Dry to a shine with a dry cloth.

To remove burned-on grease, clean with 3 to 6 drops of undiluted eucalyptus or peppermint essential oil (wear protective gloves). Wipe dry with a clean cloth.

For rust stains, first clean with a rag and a few drops of eucalyptus or peppermint essential oil. Then rub the stains with a small piece of crumpled aluminum foil, shiny side out. Wipe well with a soft cloth moistened with a mixture of 3 to 6 drops of essential oil and 1 tablespoon jojoba or almond oil.

COPPER

Decorative copper items are usually coated with lacquer to preserve the finish; they should never be polished. Only regular dusting and periodic washing are necessary. Copper cookware and utensils, on the other hand, may need special handling to remove any factory-applied lacquer. Follow the manufacturer's directions; if there aren't any instructions included, the copper pieces should be placed in a mixture of 2 gallons boiling water and 1½ cups washing soda. Let them soak until you are able to peel away the lacquer.

Stainless steel pots and pans often have copper bottoms for better distribution of heat, but high temperatures can damage them. Never scour copper bottoms with steel wool or an abrasive cleanser. If tarnishing occurs, use equal amounts of salt, flour, and vinegar to make a polishing paste.

To clean and remove tarnish from copper pots and utensils, try one of these tricks:

Citrus-salt rub. Cut a lime or lemon in half, sprinkle with salt, and rub over the copper. If you don't have any fresh lemons or limes on hand, you can use lemon juice or 1 teaspoon of any citrus essential oil mixed with 2 tablespoons water instead. Apply this solution to a damp sponge that has been sprinkled with salt. Nothing can be easier than this!

Citrus-vinegar paste. Make a paste of 1 cup vinegar, 5 drops of citrus essential oil, 1¼ cups all-purpose flour, and ½ cup salt. Spread the paste on your copper pieces and let stand for a few hours, or overnight. Then rinse, dry, and polish with a bit of olive oil to prevent further tarnishing.

Ketchup blend. Mix ½ cup ketchup with 2 tablespoons cream of tartar. Spread on the copper and let stand for an hour. Rinse in soapy water and then in clean water. Dry thoroughly.

COPPER CAUTIONS

Copper can also be vulnerable to bronze disease. Follow the suggestions given on page 115 to tackle this problem.

Pots or bowls with copper interiors cannot be used for preparing or storing acidic foods such as fruits, tomatoes, or anything containing vinegar. These foods can react with copper to form toxic compounds.

PEWTER

Antique pewter is an alloy of lead and tin. Old pewter develops a dark patina over time that looks beautiful, but due to the lead content, such pieces cannot be used to prepare or serve foods. Most pewter pieces made today are tarnish resistant, being composed of roughly 90 percent tin and 10 percent copper or antimony. This combination of metals retains its original color and is lead-free, but it is not as durable and is vulnerable to dents and scratches. Some imitation pewter pieces are made from aluminum. To be safe, check the manufacturer's instructions for the appropriate care and cleaning of individual items. Try these quick fixes for your pewter pieces:

Cabbage. Pewter can be cleaned by rubbing with wet cabbage leaves or freshly cut leaf wedges.

Minty paste. Revive dull pewter with a paste made from ¼ cup fine rottenstone, 2 teaspoons flaxseed oil, and 4 drops of peppermint or wintergreen essential oil. (Go easy — pewter is supposed to have a dark color due to its lead content.)

Salt paste. You can also clean pewter pieces with a solution of 1 teaspoon salt dissolved in 1 cup vinegar. Add 4 drops of essential oil of choice and enough all-purpose flour to make a paste. Rub onto the metal with glove-protected fingertips. Rinse well and dry thoroughly.

SILVER

Silver has many seemingly innocent enemies. Rubber, for instance, not only promotes tarnishing when in contact with silver, it can actually corrode the finish. Using rubber gloves while cleaning silver is definitely not a good idea. Likewise, avoid storing silver in rubber-lined cabinets or storage boxes. Even binding silver pieces together with rubber bands can prove detrimental.

Other substances that have a negative impact on silver include olives, eggs, salad dressing, fruit juices, vinegar, and salt. And, believe it or not, flowers should never be placed in a silver vase unless it is lined with a glass or container first. As cut flowers decompose, they release an acid that can permanently etch silver finishes.

Sterling silver is actually an alloy of approximately 92.5 percent silver and 7.5 percent copper; plated silver has a layer of silver electroplated over another metal. All silver readily oxidizes and responds to hand polishing for the best sheen and patina. The best course of action to deter tarnishing of silver flatware is to use it often, but never allow food to stand. If you can't wash it right away, rinse off any food residue until you can give your flatware a proper cleaning. (*Note:* Some decorative pieces may be lacquered; care should be taken to avoid contact with hot water.) When silver is not in use, it should be stored rolled up in a flannel cloth.

If you put your silver flatware in the dishwasher, it's best to hand-dry the items instead of letting them go through the heated drying cycle. Also, it's important to separate silver flatware from other pieces, such as stainless steel, in the silverware basket of your dishwasher to avoid scratching or possible chemical reactions with other materials.

If you have a problem with tarnish, here are a couple of formulas to try:

Easy tarnish remover. Place silver pieces in a sink or pan filled with water. Add 2 tablespoons cream of tartar and a few strips of aluminum foil. Let the silver soak for an hour or until tarnish-free. (If the silver is badly tarnished, you may notice an odor like rotten eggs. The smell is due to a chemical reaction causing the release of hydrogen sulfide gas. This gas isn't concentrated enough to be harmful, but it might be a good idea to open a window if it occurs.) Rinse silver and hand-dry all pieces with a soft cloth.

Instant tarnish remover. Squeeze some ordinary toothpaste into a small bowl and add 3 to 5 drops of peppermint or spearmint essential oil. Rub this mixture with your fingertips onto the silver. As the tarnish is removed, the toothpaste mixture will turn grayish. Rinse the silver well and hand-dry thoroughly before storing. Since gloves shouldn't be worn while cleaning silver, wash hands well when finished. If your skin begins to itch while using the cleaner, rinse well.

WHAT ABOUT GOLD?

Gold is soft metal and can easily be scratched by abrasives. The safest way to clean gold is with a paste of 1 teaspoon liquid castile soap and 1 tablespoon baking soda. Using your fingertips, gently rub the paste onto the item. Rinse in warm water and dry thoroughly with a soft cloth or towel.

CHAPTER 7

WALLS & CARPETING

DIRT AND GERMS ARE EVERYWHERE, under our feet and surrounding us on all sides. Hopefully, we don't think too much about this fact of life, or we'd start to feel a bit antsy about sitting on the floor. While cohabiting with a few germs in our life is beneficial to our health, it's probably wise to draw the line at allowing an entire eco-system from gaining a foothold in the carpeting. And who likes to look at dreary, stained walls?

Wallpaper and carpeting are really semipermanent fixtures. You can replace your living room drapes in a flash if you've grown tired of looking at them. But can you say the same about your bathroom wallpaper or den carpeting? The cost of these accessories isn't a casual matter either. It makes good sense, then, to use safe, organic products to care for your investment. Not only are they better for you and the environment, but they will help preserve the color and texture of wall coverings and carpet fibers.

Keeping Walls Clean

If you have children, fingerprints on the walls are just a part of life. Or, as the hilarious country song "Mr. Mom" points out, you may have learned the hard way that "crayons go up one drawer higher."

Walls painted with semigloss paint are the easiest to clean since they have a slick coating that doesn't absorb liquids. In fact, this type of paint is preferred for kitchens, and especially for children's rooms, where a lot can happen to a wall. Latex can also be washed, but lightly. Scrubbing and repeated application of moisture may remove not only dirt and stains but the paint as well. The best way to clean painted walls is to use a solution of equal parts vinegar and water. To a full spray bottle of solution, add 6 to 10 drops of your favorite essential oil for grease-cutting power. Just make sure to use a clear or light essential oil on walls, such as eucalyptus, mint, or tea tree. (*Note:* Tea tree oil should be used on white walls only.)

Most wallpaper made today is washable, with some even being labeled as "scrubbable." Washable papers usually have a thin film; scrubbable papers are either coated or impregnated with vinyl. In truth, you really can't scrub either one, nor should you use abrasive cleansers that could mar the paper's protective coating. The right way to clean wallpaper is to use small circular motions with a soapy cloth or sponge. The paper should then be wiped with a damp sponge and dried with a clean towel or cloth. If it becomes necessary to wash an area a second time, the paper must be allowed to dry thoroughly first. Overwetting wallpaper can cause the glue on the backing to dissolve, and soon your beautiful paper will be on the floor, not on your wall.

Wallpapered walls should be dusted frequently to reduce the risk of staining and streaking. This task is especially necessary in the kitchen and bathroom, where hot water and steam can encourage a film to develop on dirty wallpaper. If you have a wall brush attachment with your vacuum cleaner, you can use it to dust your walls. If not, an old broom or mop handle with clean rags attached to one end will suffice.

Safe & Simple Wall Formulas

The following formulas will enable you to safely clean painted walls and wallpaper. If you have a stain-removal issue and know that you have non-washable wallpaper, consult the manufacturer or check with the store where it was purchased for cleaning recommendations. Regardless of what type of paper or paint covers your walls, always test a cleaning formula on a small area for a reaction before attempting to clean the entire surface.

All-Purpose Citrus Wall Cleaner

This general formula is a good one to safely clean wall surfaces.

- **1 cup water**
- **½ cup vinegar**
- **6 drops lemon, grapefruit, or orange essential oil**

Combine all ingredients in a spray bottle. Shake vigorously before each use. Lightly spray the affected areas of your wall and wipe with a clean, damp sponge. If you're working on a stain and it's still visible after the area has completely air-dried, see the tips for cleaning walls on pages 129–131.

Disinfectant Thyme Formula

This recipe is great for cleaning wall surfaces in a child's room, as well as light switches, the sides of the crib, or wherever little fingers tend to leave smudges and germs. Use only on white walls.

- **1 cup water**
- **1 cup vinegar**
- **5 drops tea tree essential oil**
- **3 drops thyme essential oil**

Combine all ingredients in a spray bottle. Lightly spray the affected areas of your wall and wipe with a clean, damp sponge. Give a final wipe to surfaces with a sponge or cloth moistened with plain water.

THE FLOOR-TO-CEILING SOLUTION

Always clean walls by working from the bottom up to the ceiling. This advice may seem odd to you, but there is good reason for it. If you've ever tried the reverse — cleaning from top to bottom — then you've probably experienced those drip lines that travel down the wall and stay there. Those streaks of cleaning product have been working ahead of you and are very difficult to get rid of. This problem is eliminated if you take the floor-to-ceiling approach.

Minty Wall-Cleansing Paste

This cleanser is nonabrasive and will dissolve grease and fingerprints. It is recommended for use on washable papers or semigloss painted walls that are usually found in the kitchen, bathroom, and children's bedrooms. Note: The small amount of tea tree oil will not harm colored wallpaper.

¼ cup concentrated oil soap paste (available in health food and hardware stores)

2 drops peppermint essential oil

2 drops spearmint essential oil

2 drops tea tree essential oil

Put the soap paste in a short, wide-mouthed glass jar, such as a clean baby food jar. Add the essential oils and blend well. It will have the consistency of jelly. Dip a damp cloth into the soap paste and squish the cloth between your fingers to make suds. Apply to the wallpaper; rinse with another clean, damp cloth or sponge. Follow up with a dry cloth or towel.

HELPFUL HINTS FOR CLEANING WALLS

Stains and spots on nonwashable papers may be dealt with by rubbing a pencil eraser or art gum over them. The same applies to pencil marks. Or rub a freshly cut rhubarb stalk over the stain and wipe with a damp cloth. Test both methods on a small area out of view first.

Got a grease stain? Tear or cut a paper towel into four squares. To one square apply 1 or 2 drops of eucalyptus essential oil and allow it to dry. Using an iron on a low setting, press the oil-treated paper towel square against the grease stain for a few seconds. Then immediately press a clean paper towel square against the stain. Repeat this procedure with the remaining paper towel squares. If the grease stain remains, wait a few hours and apply a thick paste of cream of tartar, baking soda, and enough water to hold everything together. Brush the paste away when it has dried to a powder. If both of these methods fail, consider repainting or start shopping for new wallpaper.

Crayon scribbling on painted walls or wallpaper can be tough to tackle. Fortunately,
most crayons are washable today, but the
nonwashable type are still around. Try the
methods described above for removing grease
spots. If the crayon mark endures, and if it's
on a painted surface, scrub (yes, scrub) the
area with liquid castile soap and 1 or 2 drops
of orange essential oil. I wouldn't try this
on wallpaper (unless you think yours might
hold up), but you should be able to remove it
from a painted wall without causing too much
damage. A weathered look on the wall is better
than waxy lines of color.

Food stains, especially spaghetti sauce, always
seem to make impossible leaps from the simmering pot on the stove to the kitchen wall
several feet away (and onto everything in
between). If wiped right away, there's usually
no problem. But we never seem to notice
these stains until we go looking for them,
usually before a party or important entertain-
ing event. If the wall is covered with washable
paint or wallpaper, your task is less daunting;
just wipe it with the All-Purpose Citrus Wall
Cleaner (see page 127). If the wall is covered
with latex paint or nonwashable wallpaper,
you may have more trouble. Carefully scrape

off as much as you can with a blunt object or dull knife. If a noticeable stain remains, place 3 drops of eucalyptus essential oil on a cotton ball and then dip it in baking soda. Dab the stain with the cotton ball a few times, then rub until the stain disappears.

Deep Cleaning the Carpets?

To a lot of people, the term "deep cleaning" seems to conjure up a vision of a sea of foaming suds and water whisking away dirt from "way under." All that soapy sloshing must really get a carpet clean, right? Wrong. Too much soap and water will leave a residue in the carpet that acts like a magnet for dirt. And getting the backing of the carpet wet only creates a pool for the dirt (and stains) to collect in, not to mention promoting the potential for mildew and shrinkage of the carpet. So the first rule of carpet cleaning in terms of cleaning products is "less is more."

If you've ever steamed or shampooed your carpet by machine and have had to empty the collection tank, then you're already aware of how much gunk lives in the carpet fibers. In addition to minute pieces of sand and dead skin, there's a host of nasty critters such as mites and, if you have pets, fleas. All of these will ruin carpet fibers if given free rein. Frequent vacuuming (at least once each week) will displace these critters and their food source at the same time. Heavy traffic areas, such as hallways, stairs, and foyers, can be swept with a broom or a carpet sweeper before vacuuming. This helps to lift the nap of the carpet and bring soil to the surface for easier removal.

Do-It-Yourself Carpet Remedies

Just like the little fingerprints on our walls, footprints and spills of uncertain origin are not strangers to our wall-to-wall carpeting. Exercise the familiar "please, wipe your feet" as often as you will, but energy-driven kids in muddy sneakers often forget to pause at the doormat. This section offers some safe herbal and alternative solutions for cleaning carpets, as well as tips for treating some pretty sticky messes.

Simple Rug & Carpet Deodorizer

Pets and bare feet can cause a rather funky smell. This formula leaves your carpets looking and smelling fresh again.

- 2 **cups baking soda**
- ½ **cup cornmeal**
- 10 **drops juniper essential oil**
- 5 **drops cypress essential oil**

Combine the baking soda and cornmeal in a bowl. Add the essential oils and mix well, breaking up clumps. Sprinkle the mixture over the carpet and wait several hours, overnight if possible, before vacuuming.

Peppermint Foam Carpet Shampoo

This formula is great for cleaning heavy traffic areas.

- 3 **cups water**
- ¾ **cup vegetable-based liquid soap**
- 10 **drops peppermint essential oil**

Mix all ingredients in a blender. Rub the foam into soiled areas with a damp sponge. Let dry thoroughly and then vacuum.

Herbal Rug Restorer

Alum and vinegar combine to clean and lift carpet fibers. The essential oils leave a fresh herbal scent. Note: For spot treatment, rub a little baking soda into soiled areas. Let dry and brush clean with a soft-bristled brush. Use gloves if your hands will be coming in contact with the cleaner.

½ gallon hot water

½ cup alum

¼ cup vinegar

8 drops rosemary essential oil

3 drops lemon essential oil

Combine all ingredients in a pail or bucket. Fill a second bucket with hot water for rinsing. Dip a clean sponge mop into the vinegar solution, squeeze out excess liquid, and wipe over the carpet in sections. Rinse the mop in the second bucket between cleaning sections and squeeze out excess water. Repeat until all of the carpet has been cleaned.

Rosemary-Lavender Carpet Shampoo

This recipe makes enough for a 10- by 13-foot room. If you can't find soap flakes, you may use ¼ cup washing soda instead, but test the outcome of this substitution on a small area first.

  2 cups baking soda

  ½ cup soap flakes

  20 drops lavender essential oil

  8 drops rosemary essential oil

  ½ cup vinegar

  2 cups warm water

1. Sweep the carpet to be cleaned with a broom or carpet sweeper to loosen dirt, then vacuum the entire area. Combine the baking soda and soap flakes in a bowl. Add the essential oils and mix well, breaking up any clumps with a fork. Sprinkle the mixture on the carpet.

2. Add the vinegar to the warm water in a bucket or pail. Dip a clean sponge mop into the bucket and squeeze out as much excess liquid as you can. Gently go over the carpet with the sponge mop, working in sections. Wait at least an hour, then vacuum again.

Fleas-Be-Gone Carpet Treatment

Try this excellent formula to rid yourself of those pesky little critters. It may seem wasteful, but it's best to get rid of the vacuum cleaner bag after this treatment to prevent reinfestation of fleas.

2½ cups baking soda

10 drops sweet orange essential oil

10 drops citronella essential oil

8 drops peppermint or spearmint essential oil

6 drops lemon or lemon balm essential oil

Vacuum the carpet well. Combine all ingredients in a container and sprinkle on the carpet. Wait at least 1 hour before vacuuming again.

NATURAL CARPET STEAMER SOLUTIONS

The proportions given in the following formulas are intended for one-time use in steam carpet cleaners. Reduce or increase the volume of formula according to the type of machine you have and the amount of cleaning solution it can hold. You can also make any of these formulas in larger amounts and store for later use. Always test for colorfastness on an inconspicuous area of carpet before using a formula for the first time.

Thyme to Make Your Own Carpet Steamer Shampoo

The thyme in this formula offers antibacterial properties and a very refreshing scent. In fact, this herb received its name from the Greek word **thymon,** *which means "to fumigate."*

- ¾ cup very hot water
- ½ cup white vinegar
- 1 tablespoon liquid castile soap
- 30 drops thyme essential oil

Pour all ingredients into a container with a pour spout (or use a funnel to dispense) and blend well. Add the formula to the appropriate compartment of your steam cleaner. Clean your carpet according to the manufacturer's instructions.

A LIGHT HAND

Be careful not to saturate a carpet when using liquid cleaners, or even water. If the backing gets wet, the invading stain will have a safe place to hide, and it will be much more difficult to remove.

Heavy Duty Herbal Carpet Steamer Formula

This formula packs a punch when it comes to cutting grease and cleaning tough dirt from carpeting.

¾ cup very hot water

½ cup white vinegar

1 tablespoon hydrogen peroxide
   (omit for dark-colored carpet)

1 tablespoon liquid castile soap

1 tablespoon powdered citric acid

15 drops lemon or sweet orange essential oil

Combine all ingredients in a container or bowl. Blend well to evenly distribute the ingredients. Pour the formula into your steam cleaner and proceed to clean your carpet.

HELPFUL HINTS FOR CLEANING CARPETING

Spills should be cleaned up as soon as possible. Always blot a stain with towels or cloths to absorb excess liquid. Rubbing the stain vigorously can cause further penetration of the spill into the carpet fibers and backing.

Most food stains can be safely removed with a solution of vinegar and a bit of dishwashing soap. You can add a few drops of essential oil to the vinegar first if you like.

Blood stains and spots should be blotted with cold water or club soda. If the stain doesn't come out completely, use a cloth moistened with cold water and 2 drops of eucalyptus essential oil.

Sprinkle mud stains with salt or baking soda. Wait 30 minutes, then vacuum.

For ink stains, first cover with cream of tartar. Then take a fresh lemon wedge and squeeze a few drops of juice over the cream of tartar. Using the flesh of the lemon, gently go over the spot a few times. Brush away the powder and blot with a damp sponge.

Urine stains should first be blotted with paper towels to absorb as much of the liquid as possible. With a sponge, apply a solution of ¼ cup vinegar, 1 teaspoon dishwashing soap, and 8 to 10 drops of peppermint or eucalyptus essential oil; wait 20 minutes. (The vinegar and essential oils will help sanitize the soiled area and remove any odor.) Blot the stained area again using a clean, damp towel. *Note:* Vinegar can sometimes slightly bleach dark-colored carpets. Test this formula on an inconspicuous area first.

CHAPTER
8

CLEARING THE AIR

IN MEDIEVAL EUROPE, herbs and spices played an important role in the maintenance of the household, not only for their culinary qualities but also for their ability to mask unpleasant odors caused by poor hygiene and unsanitary conditions.

Today, although we may no longer be plagued by insufficient sanitation, we have a new challenge to face from modern household materials: Ordinary carpeting, furniture, and painted surfaces all produce toxic vapors such as VOCs (volatile organic compounds), trichloroethylene, and formaldehyde. Obviously, unless we choose to live in a tent, we cannot escape or avoid every contaminant found in building materials. But we can greatly reduce their impact on our health by purifying the air to minimize their presence in the home. How? By developing a green thumb.

Clean & Green

You may recall from high school biology that plants are involved in a process called photosynthesis. During this process, plants continuously take in carbon dioxide and other airborne toxins to produce oxygen. Bingo! You've got instant air filtration. In fact, it has been estimated that 15 to 20 spider plants will effectively detoxify a home of less than 2,000 square feet. Of course, almost any type of plant will help do the same.

If you're wondering where you are going to put all these plants, consider hanging baskets, plant stands that can hold several plants at a time, or even mini gardens on windowsills. If natural lighting is a problem, artificial lighting, such as grow lights, will keep your living air purifiers healthy. If you have little ones or pets, be sure to keep plants — especially poisonous ones — out of their reach.

Some common plants that purify air are:

* Spider plant, also known as airplane plant (*Chlorophytum comosum* 'Vittatum')
* Golden pothos (*Epipremnum aureum*)
* Peace lily (*Spathiphyllum* species)
* Fern (*Pteris* species and *Nephrolepis* species)
* Chinese evergreen (*Aglaonema* 'Silver Queen')
* Weeping fig (*Ficus benjamina*)

Herbs also filter the air, and many can easily be grown indoors year-round. Basil, thyme, oregano, sage, rosemary, mints, and geraniums are just some of the herbs that not only help clean the air but offer aromatic properties of their own, not to mention adding flavor to your favorite dishes.

Potpourri

Potpourri gets its name from a marriage of the French words *pot* (which means the same in English) and *pourri* (which means "to rot") — collectively, "rotting pot." One modern definition of potpourri is a literary or musical medley; for our purposes, it's a harmonic composition of botanical fragrances.

There is essentially no end to the different types of potpourri that you can create. All successful dried formulas require a fixative, which captures the aromatic oils from flowers, spices, and herbs when blended together. Common fixatives include orrisroot (the dried, ground rhizome of the iris plant), oakmoss, calamus root (sweet flag), benzoin gum, frankincense, cinnamon sticks, and patchouli. Fixatives can also take the form of woody material, such as pinecones, milkweed pods, and cedar shavings or chips. Some craft stores carry a fixative made from dried corncobs.

The base of a potpourri is made of dried aromatic herbs and plants, and may include flowers, stems, and leaves. Spices such as cloves, ginger, and nutmeg are also used in making potpourri blends. Fragrant herbal essential oils add concentrated aroma to potpourri and are easily obtainable. Pieces of dried bark, berries, fruit peels, and unusual seedpods are not only attractive but also act as fixatives and help preserve the scent. Bear in mind, however, that trial and error is often necessary to achieve the right balance in a potpourri, especially in its application. For instance, some potpourri ingredients may smell strong in the dry form but are lost to other ingredients that prevail when simmered in water.

It isn't necessary to add a fixative to a potpourri intended to be simmered unless you desire additional fragrance. Do not add benzoin to a simmering potpourri; although it has a nice fragrance in dried form, it is rather unpleasant when simmered. The key to making interesting potpourri blends lies in your desire to experiment, but many variations are offered here to spark your imagination.

Blending Your Own Potpourri

Making potpourri is easy. It takes moments to mix, then requires only a few seconds for a daily shake. As the weeks go on, you'll notice the scent changing, becoming mellower.

* * *

These simple steps apply to the 15 blends that follow.

1. Combine all ingredients in a wide-mouthed glass jar and stir with a spoon until well blended.
2. Cap the jar and leave it in a place free of drafts, direct sunlight, and extreme temperatures.
3. Gently shake the jar once a day for 4 to 6 weeks, or until you feel that the fragrance has fully developed.

A Midsummer's Dream

This outdoorsy potpourri may be added to pillows and sachets or set out in a dish or bowl.

- ½ cup purple basil
- ½ cup chamomile
- ½ cup marjoram
- ¼ cup yarrow (white or yellow)
- ¼ cup juniper berries
- ¼ cup oakmoss
- 2 tablespoons benzoin gum
- 2 tablespoons mace
- 1 teaspoon grated orange peel
- 15 drops cedar essential oil

Sinful Seduction

Add this potpourri to pillows and sachets or set out in a dish or bowl. Note: Tonka beans, members of the pea family, are flavorless yet contain a strong vanilla–like scent. You can find them in health food stores.

- 1 cup jasmine flowers
- 1 cup lemon verbena leaves
- ½ cup chopped gingerroot
- ½ cup clary sage leaves
- 2 tonka beans
- 1 vanilla bean, chopped into small pieces
- 1 tablespoon sandalwood chips
- 1 tablespoon cumin seed
- 20 drops patchouli essential oil

Elegant Romance

A lovely potpourri, Elegant Romance may be simmered in a pan of hot water on the stove, added to pillows and sachets, or set out in a dish or bowl.

- 1 cup rose petals
- 1 cup lavender buds
- 1 cup geranium leaves
- ½ cup lemon verbena leaves
- ½ cup powdered orrisroot
- 10 drops vanilla fragrance oil
- 8 drops sandalwood essential oil

SAVING SANDALWOOD

Sandalwood is highly valued in the perfume industry for its rich scent. The oil is extracted from the roots of a tree that can take up to 75 years to reach maturity. It doesn't grow in many places in the world, and given the current level of demand, the tree has the potential to become endangered. Always use sandalwood sparingly.

NOTE: See page 144 for basic potpourri blending instructions.

Spring Fresh

This strongly fragrant potpourri may be simmered in a pan of hot water on the stove, added to pillows and sachets, or set out in a dish or bowl.

- ½ cup rosemary leaves
- ½ cup peppermint or spearmint leaves
- ½ cup torn eucalyptus leaves
- ¼ cup thyme leaves
- ¼ cup whole cloves
- 2 teaspoons grated lemon peel
- 1 teaspoon grated orange peel

Country Roads

Simmer this autumn–scented potpourri in a pan of hot water on the stove, add it to pillows and sachets, or set it out in a pretty dish or bowl.

- 2 cups dried apple slices
- 1 cup bay leaves
- 1 cup sage
- ½ cup chopped, unpeeled gingerroot
- ½ cup whole cloves
- 8 (1-inch) cinnamon sticks

Exotic Blend

Don't simmer this blend; instead, add it to pillows and sachets, or set it out in an unusual dish or bowl.

- ½ cup jasmine flowers
- ¼ cup lemon verbena
- ¼ cup lavender
- ¼ cup sweet woodruff
- ¼ cup fennel leaves
- 2 teaspoons coriander seed
- 2 teaspoons gingerroot powder

Sweet Dreams

You can make this blend in larger quantities and sew it into herbal sleep pillows for a soothing effect. Stuff pillows and sachets with it, or set it out in a dish or bowl. You may use ¼ cup dill seed in place of the plant material.

- ½ cup chamomile flowers
- ½ cup sweet clover flowers
- ½ cup dill stems, leaves, and flowers
- ½ cup lavender flowers
- ½ cup sweet marjoram
- ¼ cup lemongrass or lemon balm leaves

NOTE: See page 144 for basic potpourri blending instructions.

FRUIT 'N' SPICE

Make old-fashioned pomanders for your closets, your cabinets, or just about anywhere. Plenty of recipes abound on the internet, using any citrus fruit and a variety of spices, but the simplest version of all is to push whole cloves into the skin of an orange until it is completely covered. If needed, thread a string or ribbon through the middle and hang. The humble pomander's benefits are many: It freshens the air, the scents remind people of the holiday season, and the smell of orange and clove drives away several common pests.

Orange Delight

This spicy potpourri may be simmered in a pan of hot water on the stove, added to pillows and sachets, or set out in a dish or bowl.

- 2 cups orange peel, cut into small strips
- 1 cup marigold flower heads
- 1 cup cubed, dried apple
- ½ cup whole cloves
- ½ cup cinnamon chips
- ½ cup calamus root
- 10 drops sweet orange essential oil

Mulberry Madness

Displaying this potpourri in a bowl or dish will catch the attention of guests. You can also add the blend to pillows or sachets.

3 cups rose petals and leaves

1 cup juniper berries

1 cup hibiscus flowers

½ cup crushed bay leaves

¼ cup star anise

2 tablespoons orrisroot

15 drops mulberry fragrance oil

    (available in craft stores)

Enchanted Hummingbird

This potpourri contains some noted hummingbird flowers. It may be added to pillows and sachets or set out in a dish or bowl.

1 cup magnolia flowers

1 cup rose hips

1 cup bee balm blossoms

1 cup lemon verbena

½ cup calendula flowers

¼ cup grated orange peel

¼ cup grated tangerine peel

2 tablespoons orrisroot

10 drops rose geranium essential oil

10 drops bergamot essential oil

Woodland Breezes

You can use this potpourri to stuff pillows and sachets, or display it in an attractive dish or bowl.

- 1 cup whole sage leaves
- 1 cup red nasturtium blossoms
- 1 cup evening primrose flowers
- 1 cup cedar chips
- ½ cup clary sage leaves
- ½ cup oakmoss
- ¼ cup chopped angelica root
- 25 drops patchouli essential oil

Morning Dew

A light, fresh blend, this potpourri may be added to pillows and sachets or set out in a dish or bowl.

- 1 cup lemon balm leaves and flowers
- 1 cup marigold blossoms
- 1 cup peppermint leaves
- ½ cup chamomile flowers
- ½ cup lemon thyme leaves
- ¼ cup grated grapefruit peel
- ¼ cup grated lemon peel
- 2 tablespoons coriander
- 1 tablespoon orrisroot
- 15 drops bergamot essential oil

NOTE: See page 144 for basic potpourri blending instructions.

Nice 'n' Spicy

Nice 'n' Spicy is a great simmering blend, but it also can be added to pillows and sachets or displayed in a dish or bowl.

- 1 cup anise hyssop
- 1 cup fennel leaves
- ½ cup pineapple-scented sage
- ¼ cup grated orange peel
- 2 tablespoons aniseed, ground
- 1 tablespoon coriander
- 1 tablespoon caraway seeds
- 10 drops sandalwood essential oil
- 5 drops vanilla essential oil

Garden Memories

This colorful blend may be added to pillows and sachets or set out in a dish or bowl.

- 1 cup calendula flowers
- 1 cup statice
- 1 cup cornflowers
- 1 cup snapdragons
- ½ cup rose petals
- ½ cup sunflower petals
- ½ cup marigolds
- ½ cup rose hips
- ½ cup juniper berries
- ¼ cup cedar chips
- ¼ cup ground anise
- 2 cinnamon sticks, crushed

Winter Blues Chaser

Have this potpourri on hand for the winter holidays. I save plenty of needles from our Christmas tree and wreath each year, so I always have a supply of balsam, cedar, or pine available. The potpourri may be simmered in a pan of hot water on the stove, added to pillows and sachets, or set out in a dish or bowl.

  1 cup evergreen needles

  ½ cup chopped dried apple

  ½ cup cedar chips

  ½ cup cinnamon sticks, broken into small pieces

  ¼ cup whole cloves

  1 tablespoon allspice berries

  1 tablespoon mace

  1 tablespoon ground cinnamon

  1 tablespoon chopped gingerroot

15 drops frankincense essential oil

10 drops myrrh essential oil

NOTE: See page 144 for basic potpourri blending instructions.

Parlor Potpourri

When it's ready, transfer the potpourri into small decorative containers and place on tables, shelves, or any other place it will be visually appreciated.

- ¾ cup non-iodized salt
- ¼ cup whole cloves
- ¼ cup allspice berries
- ¼ cup packed brown sugar
- ¼ cup crushed bay leaves
- 1 cup rose petals
- 1 cup hydrangea petals
- ½ cup dried rose geranium leaves
- ½ cup lavender flowers
- ½ cup dried and crumbled rosemary sprigs
- ¼ cup crushed bay leaves
- ¼ cup orrisroot
- 2 tablespoons cognac

1. Combine the salt, cloves, allspice, brown sugar, and bay leaves in a bowl. In a separate bowl, mix the remaining ingredients except the cognac. Place some of this mixture in a widemouthed jar or crock and sprinkle with some of the salt mixture. Continue alternating layers in this manner, ending with a layer of the salt mixture.

2. Sprinkle the cognac over all and place a heavy rock on top to weigh the mixture down. Tightly seal the jar or crock. Stir this mixture once a day for 4 to 6 weeks, replacing the weight each time. If the mixture dries out, add a bit more cognac.

Herbal Mists

It's really quite simple to have an herbal spray air freshener available for every room of your home. It's a lot of fun to create unique blends that help eliminate unpleasant odors while expressing the real you.

As a bonus, some sprays can perform double duty. For instance, in the kitchen, a small spray bottle of distilled water and thyme essential oil can be used to tame pungent cooking odors and as a wash for fruits and vegetables. Spray the produce and gently scrub with a vegetable brush. Rinse well in clean water.

Decorative cobalt glass bottles are a great choice if the herbal mist will be in view. Of course, you can use almost any spray bottle or even a plant mister.

To make your own herbal spray air freshener, first wash the container thoroughly. Then fill it with water and add 5 to 7 drops of an essential oil or combination of oils per 8 ounces water. (Use distilled water if it's also going to come in contact with human skin or foods; do not spray on skin within 12 hours of exposure to sun.) Some suggested blends are on the following page.

BLEND	ESSENTIAL OILS
Country Spice	Cinnamon, ginger, vanilla, bay
Spring Morning	Lavender, rose, geranium, rosemary, sweet orange
Earthy	Sage, thyme, cedar, patchouli, frankincense
Romance	Vanilla, sandalwood, ylang-ylang, jasmine, neroli, rose
Far East	Patchouli, cedar, sandalwood, lime, coriander
Energizing	Basil, lavender, orange, nutmeg, mint
Calming	Bergamot, geranium, clary sage, chamomile, yarrow
Gardener's Parade	Lemon, orange, basil, thyme

Simple Sachets

Sachets made from dried herbs and flowers will keep your linens and clothing smelling sweet while keeping insects at bay. A sachet formula doesn't need to be complicated to be effective — just a few ingredients are all that's required. In fact, if you don't have any dried herbs or flowers available, you can stuff the sachet with a bit of moss or even polyester fill scented with essential oil.

Sachets can be made in just minutes by stitching a double-layered square of cheesecloth, muslin, or scrap of fabric on three sides and tying with a ribbon. You can also make use of those socks that mysteriously return mateless from the laundry room;

socks are ideal holders for sachets to scent sneakers, boots, and shoes.

These are some of my favorite ways to use sachets:

* Hang them in clothes closets or coat closets.
* Place them in dresser drawers.
* Use them to keep seasonal clothes fresh when being stored, such as in a trunk or storage closet.
* Put some in your sneakers, gardening shoes, or any other regularly used shoes.
* Tuck them under sheets and towels in the linen closet.

Spiced Sachets

This recipe has a zesty aroma and is especially nice to use around the holidays to scent linens for guests. You'll have enough filling for two to four sachets.

2 cups cinnamon chips

½ cup whole cloves

½ cup whole peppercorns

½ cup dried gingerroot slices

2 tablespoons ground cinnamon

1 tablespoon aniseed

2 teaspoons caraway seed

Combine all ingredients in a bowl and mix by hand or with a spoon to blend. Place spoonfuls of the blend onto muslin or cloth squares, leaving enough room to sew the sides together.

Deserving Drawers

This recipe is great to use in sock and sweater drawers. It lends a long-lasting earthy scent. Makes four to six sachets.

- 3 cups cedar chips
- 2 cups oakmoss
- 1 cup sandalwood chips
- 1 cup dried sage
- 1 vanilla bean, crushed
- 15 drops patchouli essential oil

Combine the cedar, oakmoss, sandalwood, and sage in a glass or ceramic bowl. Mix with a wooden spoon. Add the vanilla bean and essential oil and stir until completely mixed. Place spoonfuls of the blend onto muslin or cloth squares, leaving enough room to sew the sides together.

Sweet Linens Sachet

This sachet recipe imparts a sweet aroma to linens and towels. Remember, all herbal materials should be dried before using in sachets. Depending on the size of the squares, this recipe will make four to six sachets.

- 4 **cups oakmoss**
- 2 **cups rosemary leaves and flowers**
- 2 **cups lavender leaves and flowers**
- ½ **cup lemon balm or lemon verbena**
- 1 **tablespoon orrisroot**
- 0 **drops lavender essential oil**
- 6 **drops rosemary essential oil**

Combine the dried herbs in a glass or ceramic bowl. Add the orrisroot and stir with a wooden spoon. Add the essential oils and mix well. Place spoonfuls of the blend onto muslin or cloth squares, leaving enough room to sew the sides together. Place the sachets on shelves or hang inside linen closets and cupboards.

Mentholated Sneaker Tamer

Here's another odor-absorbing recipe to make your sneakers less unruly. Be sure to use only dried herbs in your potpourris.

- 2 cups natural clay cat litter
- 1 cup baking soda
- 1 cup calendula flowers
- 1 cup peppermint or spearmint leaves
- ½ cup thyme leaves
- 10 drops peppermint essential oil
- 10 drops wintergreen essential oil
- 10 drops eucalyptus essential oil

Combine the cat litter and baking soda in a glass or ceramic bowl and mix with a wooden spoon. Add the herbs and mix again. Add the essential oils and blend. Place half of the mixture in each of two clean socks and tie the open ends shut. Place a stuffed sock in each sneaker overnight or when not in use.

Sage Citrus Sneaker Tamer

If your sneakers advertise the fact that you've been working hard,
this recipe will help you keep the news to yourself.

- **2 cups dried sage**
- **1½ cups dried lemon balm**
- **2 cups cedar chips**
- **½ cup baking soda**
- **2 tablespoons grated orange peel**
- **10 drops rosemary essential oil**
- **5 drops lemon essential oil**

Combine the dried herbs, cedar chips, baking soda, and orange peel in a glass or ceramic bowl. Stir with a wooden spoon. Add the essential oils and stir to blend. Place half of the mixture in a clean sock and tie the open end shut. Stuff another sock with the remaining mixture and tie off. Place a stuffed sock in each sneaker overnight or when not in use.

MORE FRAGRANT IDEAS

Don't limit yourself to the three main types of air fresheners discussed here — be creative!

Hang dried herbs in closets and storage rooms to deter insects. Some good choices are mints, rosemary, lavender, sage, lemongrass, and citronella.

Make vacuuming a sweeter experience: Place a few drops of essential oil on the outside of the filter bag of your vacuum cleaner.

If you have a fireplace, place 2 or 3 drops of essential oil of choice on the wood before lighting.

Add a few drops of a citrus essential oil to your humidifier. Do not use essential oils for this purpose if you suffer from asthma, however.

Add 1 or 2 drops of essential oil to a diffuser ring made to attach to the bulb of a standing lamp. The heat of the bulb will release the fragrance when the lamp is in use. Don't allow the essential oil to come in direct contact with the bulb; this can cause the bulb to explode and could result in a fire.

THE GARAGE & BASEMENT

THE GARAGE AND BASEMENT ARE TWO PLACES where one is most likely to find the largest collection of solvents, paints, and various household chemicals. How do you safely and responsibly dispose of them?

The first rule of greening your garage and basement is to know what not to do. Do not, under any circumstances, pour these products down the drain, dump them outside, or send them to the landfill. Doing any of these things would be detrimental to the local groundwater and wildlife, as well as home septic systems.

The next step is to find out if your town or city has a collection program for hazardous waste materials. Your refuse and recycling collection provider may be able to provide this information or may have a program of its own. If you need more help, check out Earth911.com, where you can learn how to dispose of everything from automotive products to electronics just by entering your zip code.

Walls & Floors

You may think it's silly to clean the walls and floors of a garage or basement, but these areas can take on unpleasant odors and invading pathogens such as mold and mildew. And if the garage or basement is used for recreation or work, you'll especially appreciate the removal of these unwelcome visitors. The following formulas are made from simple ingredients, and they are as effective as they are easy to use.

Mold & Mildew Destroyer

This formula works well on concrete floors and walls made of cinder block. Try it out in your garage or your basement. Note: A string mop works best on cinder–block walls because their texture tends to tear sponge mop heads.

> ½ gallon water
> 2 cups hot vinegar
> 1 cup lemon juice
> 2 teaspoons tea tree essential oil

Combine all ingredients in a large bucket. Dip a mop into the bucket and wring out excess liquid. Wipe the walls from the top down. Do not rinse. You can also wash concrete floors with this solution. If there are windows in the room, open them and let everything air-dry for a few hours.

Oil Spill Remover

If you're fortunate enough to be able to park your car in the garage, then one thing is certain: You will have occasional oil leaks or spills on the garage floor. Try this trick to remove the oil and its telltale odor.

> 2 **cups natural cat litter**
> ½ **cup baking soda**
> 8 **drops eucalyptus or peppermint essential oil**

Combine all ingredients in a small bucket or pail. Sprinkle the mixture over the oil spill and let stand for 2 to 3 days. Then just sweep up the powder.

HELPFUL HINTS FOR STORAGE AREAS

Remove stale smells from freezers and ice chests by wiping the interior walls with equal parts water and white vinegar, followed by a second wipe with a clean cloth sprinkled with a few drops of essential oil of your choice, or vanilla extract.

Control excessive moisture in your basement by setting out a few bowls of charcoal pellets (not barbecue charcoal bricks). If you can't find charcoal pellets, clay or kitty litter will work, too.

Clean up mildewed books by sprinkling cornstarch that has been mixed with 1 to 2 drops of tea tree essential oil on the soiled pages. After a few hours, wipe the pages clean with a dry cloth.

Caring for Tools

To keep garden tools in good working order, they should be clean and dry before storing. Use a wire brush to remove dirt, and wipe tools with a dry cloth if they have any mud or moisture on them.

Tool Conditioner

Large tools like shovels and rakes should be stored in this mixture to prevent rusting.

> **1 quart olive oil**
> **bucket of sand**

Mix the oil into the bucket of sand. Push large tools headfirst into the mixture and leave there when not in use.

South of the Border Rust Remover

Here's a simple, fragrant, and nontoxic way to remove rust from your tools.

> **table salt**
> **juice from one lime**

Sprinkle table salt directly on the tool, covering the rusty area completely. Sprinkle the juice from a freshly cut lime over the salt until saturated. Find something else to do for about 3 hours, then come back and wipe the rust-free tool clean.

HELPFUL HINTS FOR TOOL MAINTENANCE

A peg board is a big tool-storing help in the garage. And if you outline your tools on the board with a pencil, you'll know when something is missing, and what to look for.

Paint the handles of your tools a bright color, such as yellow or red. That way they'll be seen before they're stepped on or hit by the lawnmower.

Old tools can be recycled by turning them into garden ornaments. I use an old push broom handle to support a weather vane in one of my flower gardens. Antique tools can be displayed as a collection on the wall of a den or workshop. Just use your imagination!

Clean Your Car Naturally

Even your automobiles can be cared for without the use of the toxic products currently sold for this purpose. The following formulas can be applied to your car, truck, boat, or recreational vehicle. Wear protective gloves when using these mixtures.

Easy Citrus Car Wash

This extremely simple formula is all you need to get your car clean.

1 gallon water

¼ cup liquid castile soap

10 drops lemon or orange essential oil

Fill a bucket with the water and soap, and stir until mixed. Add the essential oil and stir again. Using a soft cloth or sponge, wash the exterior of your car from the top down, one section at a time. Rinse each area well with clean water before the soap has a chance to dry.

Get-Tough-to-Get-Dirt-Going Formula

This formula is for added shine and to remove really tough dirt and grime.

    1 gallon water
    ½ cup lemon juice
    6 drops eucalyptus or mint essential oil
    ¼ cup liquid castile soap
    3 tablespoons baking soda

Mix the water, lemon juice, essential oil, and soap in a bucket. Add the baking soda and stir until blended. With a soft cloth or sponge, wash the exterior of your car from the top down, working in sections. Rinse each area well with clean water before the soap dries.

Tire Wash

Use this cleaner to keep your tires looking like new.

    2 cups baking soda
    ½ cup water
    ¼ cup liquid castile soap
    2 cups vinegar or lemon juice
    5 drops lemon, lime, or orange essential oil

Combine the baking soda, water, and soap in a bucket or other container. Add the vinegar and essential oil, and mix well. Apply with a brush to get in between the tire treads. Wash one tire at a time, rinsing each before moving on to the next.

Headlight Scrub

This formula will easily remove grime and the remains of insects that have met their end on your headlights.

> ¼ cup baking soda
> 1½ tablespoons liquid castile soap
> 8 drops eucalyptus or pine essential oil

Combine all ingredients in a bowl and mix well. Dip a cloth, brush, or sponge into the wash and scrub each headlight. Rinse several times with a wet cloth or sponge or with a garden hose.

Herbal Car Wax

An all-natural recipe, this wax really protects your car's finish. It can be made in larger quantities and stored.

> 3 tablespoons beeswax
> 3 tablespoons carnauba wax flakes
> 1 cup flaxseed oil
> 6 drops orange or lemon essential oil
> ½ cup lemon juice

1. Melt the waxes and flaxseed oil together in the top of a double boiler, stirring often. Add the essential oil, stir once, and immediately remove from the heat.
2. Pour the mixture into a clean coffee can. (*Note:* The can will become hot.) Using gloves or potholders, place the coffee can in a place where it will be undisturbed for a few days.

3. When the wax has completely hardened, tap the sides of the can until the wax breaks free. Turn out the wax and rub it directly on your car.
4. Dip a soft cloth into the lemon juice and squeeze dry. Polish the waxed car with the lemon juice–soaked cloth, then buff to a shine with a dry cloth.

Fresh-Scent Vinyl Upholstery Cleaner

If you're sensitive to that new-car smell, this formula will help eliminate it.

- **2 tablespoons baking soda**
- **2 cups hot water**
- **1 teaspoon orange, cedar, or mint essential oil**

Dissolve the baking soda in the hot water in a bucket. Blend in the essential oil. Vacuum the upholstery to remove loose dirt and debris from crevices and between the seats. (Watch out for loose change!) Moisten a soft cloth with the formula and rub over the upholstery, working from the top down. Rinse with a clean, damp cloth, then dry to a shine with a dry towel.

Lavender Leather Upholstery Cleaner

To safely clean leather and impart a light lavender scent, try this formula. After cleaning, apply Fragrant Leather Upholstery Conditioner (below).

- ¼ cup soap flakes
- 1 cup hot water
- 6 drops mint or lavender essential oil

Dissolve the soap flakes in the hot water. Add the essential oil and blend. Apply this formula with a soft brush, using gentle downward strokes. Wipe with a clean, damp cloth. Buff dry with a towel.

Fragrant Leather Upholstery Conditioner

Use this conditioner after cleaning your leather upholstery with Lavender Leather Upholstery Cleaner (above). The olive oil and rosemary tea will keep leather seats soft and conditioned.

- ½ cup olive oil
- ¾ cup vinegar
- 20 drops lavender essential oil

Combine all ingredients in a spray bottle and shake well. Lightly spray onto the upholstery and buff with a dry cloth.

Quick Chrome Cleaner

If there are a lot of stains or bugs stuck on the chrome parts of your car, you can use a nylon-backed sponge with this formula. Make your own nylon sponge by securing a square of onion bag netting over a clean sponge or cloth. Note: Use a squirt bottle for this recipe, since the mixture may clog the nozzle of a spray bottle.

- ½ cup baking soda
- ¼ cup lemon juice
- 3 drops citrus essential oil of choice

Combine the baking soda and lemon juice in a squirt bottle. Add the essential oil and shake well. Apply directly to chrome and wipe with a damp cloth. Rinse with clean water.

Dashboard Restorer

This simple formula will make your dashboard look brand new again.

- 1 cup water
- ½ cup vegetable oil–based soap (such as Murphy's)
- 10 drops cedar essential oil

Combine all ingredients in a small spray bottle and shake well. Spray onto the dashboard and wipe clean with a soft cloth.

Tar Solvent

This formula is for those specks of tar that land on your car after driving on a freshly paved road.

- **1 tablespoon lemon juice or vinegar**
- **2 teaspoons lemon essential oil**
- **4 drops tea tree essential oil**

Mix all ingredients in a small bowl. Rub some of the solution into the tar with glove-protected fingertips or a sponge to loosen. Allow the formula to remain on the tar for 15 minutes, then wipe or scrape the remaining tar off with a nylon-backed sponge.

Window Wash

In winter, this formula helps reduce frost buildup.

- **3 cups vinegar**
- **1 cup water**
- **10 drops lemon essential oil**

Combine all ingredients in a large spray bottle and shake well. Spray liberally onto windows and wipe clean with a chamois cloth.

Mat & Carpet Cleaner

Even if you've cleaned your car inside and out, dingy mats and carpeting will spoil the effect. This solution not only cleans those items but also makes them smell fresh again.

- ½ **gallon hot water**
- ½ **cup liquid castile soap**
- 12 **drops wintergreen or peppermint essential oil**

1. Combine all ingredients in a bucket or pail. Stir thoroughly to mix.
2. Vacuum loose any dirt from the carpeting and mats. Remove the mats from the car and clean by dipping a brush into the cleaning solution and rubbing it into the carpet fibers. Rinse the mats with a hose and allow them to dry in the sun.
3. Clean the carpeting on the floor of the car by dipping a brush into the cleaning solution and rubbing it into the carpet. Wipe with a dry towel. Vacuum again when completely dry.

CLEANING SEASONAL VEHICLES

Here's a way to tackle musty odors from campers, boats, and motor homes that haven't been in use for long periods of time. Fill a small bowl with a little white vinegar and a few drops of essential oil, if you wish. Add a piece of bread on top of the liquid and place the bowl inside the vehicle to absorb odors. Remove the bowl after 24 hours.

Instant Herbal Car Deodorizer

If your pets frequently travel in the car, then you know how odors can linger long after the ride is over. This formula will eliminate those odors.

- ¾ cup water
- ¼ cup vinegar
- 6 drops lavender essential oil
- 4 drops lemon essential oil
- 4 drops sweet orange essential oil
- 2 drops peppermint essential oil

Combine all ingredients in a small spray bottle (about 8 ounces) and shake well. Hold the spray bottle 6 to 8 inches from surfaces and lightly mist the upholstery and carpeting. Leave the car windows and doors open for 15 minutes after spraying, if possible. Don't let Fido back into the car immediately, as the essential oils can irritate his paws and sensitive nose.

Sweet Summer Sachet

This fragrant sachet is simple to make, although some of these essential oils deviate from the standard ones used for cleaning. Vetiver has a lovely, warm, exotic aroma that pairs beautifully with orange and vanilla. Ginger adds a spicy note. If you make your own perfumes and personal body–care products, then you probably already have these oils in your inventory.

2 (4-inch) squares of fabric

1 (3-inch) square of cotton batting, or 6 cotton balls

10 drops sweet orange essential oil

10 drops vetiver essential oil

8 drops pure vanilla extract

6 drops ginger essential oil

1. Place one fabric square on a flat surface, pattern-side down. On top of this, place the cotton batting or cotton balls. Add the essential oils and extract to the cotton and place the remaining square of fabric, pattern-side up, on top.

2. Stitch or use a hot glue gun to seal the edges of the fabric squares. Attach a loop or strand of ribbon at the top and hang it from your rearview mirror.

Fruity Travel Wipes

These travel wipes are quick and easy to make. They sure come in handy, too!

10 (5- by 8-inch) pieces of cellulose sponge cloth or cotton
    T-shirt
10 drops lemon essential oil
10 drops sweet orange essential oil
 6 drops lime essential oil
 2 drops tea tree essential oil

1. Fold each piece of cloth in half and place in a ziplock bag or a small container with an airtight lid. Add enough water to saturate each cloth, but not enough to cover them.
2. Press down on the cloths with one hand and drain the excess water into a cup. Add the remaining ingredients to the water in the cup and stir. Pour this mixture over the cloths and seal the container.
3. Keep the container in the glove compartment of your car and use a wipe when needed to clean hands and face.

Sudden Spill & Spot Remover

It never fails — someone spills ice cream or soda on the floor or upholstery just as you've pulled onto the highway. This formula will lift out most stains, including those left by greasy foods, and leave a fresh, clean smell.

- ½ **cup vinegar**
- ½ **cup club soda**
- 8 **drops eucalyptus essential oil**
- 3 **drops wintergreen essential oil**

Combine all ingredients in a small spray bottle and shake well. Spray directly onto the stain and blot with a clean, dry cloth. Repeat as necessary.

EMERGENCY CARE FOR MOTION SICKNESS

If someone in your family is prone to car sickness, you don't want to be without this simple remedy! Place 2 or 3 drops of peppermint or ginger essential oil on a tissue. Sniff the tissue until the feeling passes. Although this treatment usually works well for people, I can't be sure about its effect on the family dog.

Under-the-Hood Maintenance

You didn't think you'd see any herbal formulas in this department, did you? In truth, there aren't many, but what is presented here is useful nonetheless. These formulas can be used on the engine of your car, lawnmower, or other machinery.

Engine Degreaser

A buildup of oil and grease on an engine can adversely affect performance and could result in an engine fire. Cut through grease with this powerful cleaner.

> ¼ cup washing soda
>
> 1 cup water
>
> 1 cup vinegar
>
> 25 drops tea tree essential oil
>
> 20 drops citrus essential oil of choice

1. Pour the washing soda into a jug or pitcher, one with a tight-fitting cap and preferably a pour spout.

2. Bring the water and vinegar to a boil in a saucepan. Remove from the heat and add to the jug. Cap the jug and shake to dissolve the washing soda. (Careful — it will be hot!) Add the essential oils and shake once more.

3. Slowly pour the solution over a cool engine (one that has not been run for at least an hour). Use a stiff brush to loosen oil and grease. Rinse with a garden hose or pour clean water over the engine several times. Leave the engine exposed to the air until completely dry.

Battery Terminal Cleaner

Battery terminals can develop a lot of gunk over time, leading to corrosion and a shortened life for your battery.

½ cup baking soda
4 drops lime or orange essential oil
water

Combine all ingredients in a small bowl or cup and blend well, using only enough water to make a paste of medium thickness. Apply the paste to battery terminals with an old toothbrush and scrub until clean. Wipe the terminals clean with a slightly damp cloth, then wipe again with a dry cloth.

Corrosion Resistance for Battery Terminals

To keep unsightly battery corrosion from happening, use this simple formula. Note: The paintbrush you use can be restored by soaking it in hot vinegar.

½ tablespoon 100% pure aloe vera gel
1 tablespoon petroleum jelly

Mix the aloe vera gel and petroleum jelly together in a cup. Apply the mixture to the battery terminals with the tip of a small paintbrush.

Radiator Rescue

This formula has two parts. Use the wash for the exterior of your car radiator, then follow with the finishing treatment to deter rust.

TO WASH:

2 cups boiling water

¾ cup washing soda

6 drops rosemary essential oil

TO FINISH:

1 cup water

2 teaspoons pure linseed oil

1. Combine the wash ingredients in a bowl or other container; stir to mix. Pour over a cool radiator and use a brush to clean off any oil or grease residue.
2. Rinse with clean water and allow the radiator to air-dry.
3. Combine the finish ingredients in a small spray bottle and shake well. Lightly spray the radiator. Allow to air-dry before using the vehicle.

GASKET & HOSE MAINTENANCE

Protect gaskets and hoses from cracking in extreme temperatures: Pour a few table-spoons of olive oil into a cup, then dip the tip of a small paintbrush into the oil and shake off any excess. Apply to rubber hoses and gaskets, and also door seals. Go over these areas again with a dry cloth to remove excess oil.

chapter 10

THE GARDEN & LANDSCAPE

PERSONALLY, I REGARD MY YARD, DECK, AND GARDENS as extensions of my home, even though they are seasonal territories. And because we have several "fur-kids" in the form of three cats herded by an Australian shepherd, it is absolutely essential to maintain a safe and healthy outdoor environment.

Unfortunately, your outdoor living spaces can become vulnerable to unwelcome intrusions, including mildew on your outdoor accoutrements and pests in your plants. The good news is that it's perfectly possible to exercise as much care for the exterior of your home as the interior, and do it as naturally as possible to reduce your environmental impact.

From the following pages, you'll discover how to make and use natural formulas to care for brick, decking, siding, wicker furniture, and even your outdoor grill. You'll also learn how to safely and effectively convince unwanted garden visitors to find greener pastures.

Decks, Patios & Exterior Siding

One of the easiest and most effective methods to clean these types of surfaces is a good washing with a pressure washer. However, if you don't have access to one, or have some tough stains that stubbornly remain even after pressure washing, then try one of these advanced solutions.

Fill the pressure washer tank with equal parts water and white vinegar. You may also add 1 tablespoon powdered citric acid for each cup of liquid, if you wish.

Oxalic acid is an organic substance that occurs naturally in many plants, most notably tea (*Camellia sinensis*), sorrel, buckwheat, and rhubarb, as well as in most berries and certain fruits. Used to bleach wood decking and remove mildew, rust, and other stains, it is available from most hardware stores and home centers as dry crystals that are reconstituted in water. However, being a caustic acid, it's also highly corrosive, and great care should be taken to protect your skin and eyes, as well as taking precautions to prevent children and pets from coming into contact with this material.

Wicker Furniture

Wicker refers to the art of weaving a variety of plant-based fibers to lend form and structure, a practice that dates back to ancient Egypt. The base material may be wood, vine, or rush. As furniture, wicker is durable yet light, making it a very portable and suitable decor for porches, covered patios, and sunrooms.

Today, some so-called wicker furnishings are actually made from plastic, and if your outdoor furniture is this type, cleaning it is an easy task. An occasional wipe down with a damp cloth is all that's needed. However, other types of wicker require a different method of cleaning. For instance, wood- and vine-based wicker needs some humidity to keep it from cracking, while wicker made from paper-fiber rush cannot tolerate moisture at all. For this reason, try to determine what kind of wicker you have. If you can't, or if your wicker is painted, then stick to cleaning it with a vacuum hose or a dry cloth.

BOTTOM'S UP TIP FOR WICKER
Sometimes, wicker seats can sag with age and frequent use. To remedy this, spray the wicker (wood or rattan only) completely with plain water. Then set the furniture in the sun to dry. This will help the wicker bands tighten.

Weekend Warrior Wicker Wash

If you know that your wicker is wood based, you can go to town cleaning it with this formula without being concerned about getting it wet. The essential oils used here will dissolve grime, while the gentle soap will make its removal easier.

1 gallon water

1 tablespoon liquid castile soap (or Murphy's Oil Soap)

20 drops cedar essential oil

10 drops sweet orange oil

Combine all ingredients in a pail of water. Dip a soft cloth or cellulose sponge into the cleaning solution, squeeze out the excess liquid, and wipe down the wicker using even strokes from top to bottom. Wipe a second time with a clean, dry cloth. Let the furniture dry completely before using it again, usually for several hours.

Lemony Wicker Conditioning Treatment

This technique may be used to restore wood- or vine-based wicker.

1½ cups hot water

20 drops lemon essential oil

¼ cup flaxseed oil

Combine the hot water and essential oil in a spray bottle and gently shake to mix. Apply this solution to clean wicker and allow the item to dry in the sun. When dry, apply a very light coating of the flaxseed oil using a clean, dry cloth. After a day or two, the oil will be absorbed. If any residue remains, simply wipe the wicker with a dry cloth before using the furniture again.

Cleaning Stone & Brick

Dirt, spills, grease, and soot can affect the function and appearance of stone and brick objects, such as barbecue pits, retaining walls, patio flooring, and chimineas (freestanding fireplaces). Here's how to keep these items looking and performing at their best.

TERRA-COTTA CARE TIPS

* Put a coffee filter (preferably unbleached) in the bottom of your terra-cotta pots before planting to prevent soil loss and staining of your deck flooring and railings.
* Place small seashells in pots, upside down, to help capture and retain moisture between watering.
* To help keep terra-cotta pots looking clean and new, coat them inside and out with a light layer of flaxseed or olive oil.

Give Up the Grime Degreaser

Washing soda is a natural degreaser, and camphor essential oil is employed as a solvent in the paint industry. If you can't find this essential oil at your local health food store, look for an online supplier. It's inexpensive, and a little goes a long way.

- **1** gallon hot water
- **½** cup washing soda
- **30** drops white camphor essential oil

Combine all ingredients in a pail or bucket. Dip a scrub brush into the cleaning solution and apply to the brick or stone surface and scrub (wearing gloves is recommended). Once the entire surface has been cleaned, rinse thoroughly with a garden hose.

Barbecue Grills

Grills typically get a lot of use during the summer months, and some people use them all year long. Spills and grease marks are bound to happen. Frequent but gentle cleaning will help to protect the finish and your investment.

Stainless Steel Barbecue Polish

Wipe this solution on your grill's exterior for lots of shine.

- ½ cup water
- 4–5 teaspoons baking soda
- 10 drops lavender essential oil

Combine the water and just enough baking soda to make a thin paste — it should be goopy, not too thick. Add the essential oil and blend well. Apply the paste onto your grill using circular motions with a soft cloth. Rinse with either plain water or a solution of equal parts water and white vinegar. Finish by drying and buffing the stainless steel with a dry cloth.

Pest-Free Garden Parties

Once you've cleaned your deck, your outdoor furniture, and your grill, you'll want to enjoy your yard without being bugged by bugs. To keep ants from spoiling your picnic, sprinkle a mixture of salt and ground cinnamon around the area. If your bug problems are in the air rather than on the ground, hang strips of ribbon or cloth, moistened with several drops of lavender essential oil, from nearby trees or other stationary fixtures to deter flying insects. Other natural fly-repellent strategies include placing a bowl of lemon or orange peels on the table or using the Shoo-Fly Shake below.

Shoo-Fly Shake

Place a few small bowls outside, filled with the following combination of dried herbs, to keep flies away from your backyard barbecue or afternoon tea party.

2 cups lavender flowers

1 cup rosemary

1 cup southernwood

½ cup spearmint

¼ cup mugwort

¼ cup cedar chips

3 heaping tablespoons orrisroot

Combine all ingredients in one or more bowls and distribute as needed.

Pest Patrol & Control

Pests come in an assorted variety — some with roots and others with tails; some may be merely bothersome, while others can be downright destructive. All of them can affect your enjoyment of your outdoor landscape. Worse yet, some of these pests need to be dealt with outside before they have the opportunity to take up residence inside your home.

Before you can control common pests, you must first patrol to see where your home and property may be vulnerable to entry. Cracks around windows and doors should be sealed. If you find any holes intended for electrical or plumbing coming into the house that a mouse or other creature could slip into, fill up the excess space with steel wool. Inspect your garden plants, trees, and shrubs for signs of unwelcome visitors, such as aphids or fungus. Once you've completed your rounds and taken notes, you'll be ready to take control of your outdoor living space.

STRUGGLING WITH WEEDS

What distinguishes a weed from a valid garden plant is a personal choice for each gardener. Some people deliberately harvest and even cultivate dandelions, for instance, to make dandelion wine or fritters (try them both sometime!). Others consider this prolific plant to be a pesky nuisance. In any case, you'll want to refrain from using toxic chemicals to prevent any unwanted flora from encroaching upon your lawn or garden areas.

Corn gluten, a by-product from corn milling, is an organic lawn care control valued for its effectiveness as both a lawn food and a weed deterrent. Corn gluten works as a natural plant food because it delivers nitrogen. At the same time, however, it prevents germination of invading weeds by robbing the seed of moisture as soon as it sprouts. This preemergent ability not only helps rid your lawn of dandelions but also addresses some other persistent invaders, such as purslane and crabgrass.

Corn gluten is available as a fine powder, as pellets, or in granular form, the latter being the easiest to distribute via a spreader. Many garden centers carry this product in stock. However, some of you may need to order it online. In either case, be sure to follow the directions on the package to ensure proper application and watering to activate this double-duty weed and feed.

Homemade Herbal Herbicide

This formula is highly effective at eradicating unwanted lawn and garden dwellers, including poison ivy. However, it will also kill any plant that comes in contact with it, so be careful where you spray it. Note: Herbal extracts are not the same thing as essential oils. Extracts are liquids that are distilled from raw plant material using alcohol. They are readily available online.

2 cups white vinegar

½ cup salt

¼ cup powdered citric acid

¼ cup witch hazel extract

2 teaspoons lavender extract

2 teaspoons chamomile extract

¼ cup wheat germ oil

1. Heat the white vinegar in a medium saucepan until it just comes to a boil. (You might want to open the windows first.)
2. Remove from the heat and add the salt, stirring well to dissolve. Add the remaining ingredients, and stir again.
3. Using a funnel, pour the solution into a large spray bottle.
4. Spray the solution directly onto the weed, including the base near the roots. If possible, try to apply the solution while it's still hot for best results.

Horsetail Garden Tea

Horsetail is abundant in silica, making this herb's properties beneficial to garden plants as a nutrient, as well as being an excellent deterrent for mildew and other fungi.

1 gallon water

1 cup dried horsetail (leaves and stems)

Bring the water to a boil, then add the horsetail. Reduce the heat and simmer the brew for 20 minutes. Strain and pour the reserved infusion into a spray bottle. Allow the solution to cool completely before spraying liberally on and around your plants.

GOT MILKY SPORE?

This excellent organic product solves several problems at once and will keep on working for up to 40 years! Milky spore is a naturally occurring friendly bacteria for lawns. This natural treatment is lethal to grubs, which are actually the larvae of Japanese beetles, a common and harmful garden pest that feeds on grass, flowers, fruits — just about anything that grows out of the ground. By getting rid of the grubs, you'll not only be reducing the Japanese beetle population, you will also be removing the primary food source for another destructive visitor — the mole. Best of all, milky spore won't harm the surrounding soil, grass, or your children and pets.

You might be able to find this product at your local garden center. If not, check for an online supplier. It's not very expensive and it goes a long way — a 10-ounce container will cover about 2,500 square feet. The spores continue to self-propagate, too, even lying dormant over long periods of time until an unsuspecting grub enters the scene. This endurance is why it's so effective for so long.

FRIENDLY FUNGICIDES

While not exactly friendly to pests and disease, there are some organic elementals and minerals that are far less toxic than standard pesticides and fungicides. If you have a severe problem with black spot or powdery mildew running rampant among your plants, you might want to consider using one of these materials.

Keep in mind that even though the following agents may be naturally occurring, you still need to exercise caution while using them: Be sure you follow all package directions and recommended precautions very carefully.

Copper sulfate and elemental sulfur are both accepted by organic gardening standards and are very effective against forms of mildew, black spot, damping-off (a viral disease that affects seedlings), arthropods, and mites. These materials work by altering the pH on the surface of the vegetation, rendering it unsuitable to sustain fungal growth. In addition, these agents disrupt the metabolic processes of insects, which inhibits reproduction. *Caution:* Sulfur and sulfur compounds are corrosive to metal.

Diatomaceous earth (DE) is applied as a powder, which is composed of crushed fossils. Nontoxic to humans, DE keeps the population levels of many lawn residents — such as grubs, slugs, and fleas — in check. One caveat: DE will also kill beneficial insects on your lawn, such as nematodes. For this reason, you may want to use DE only in the infested area rather than broadcast it across the entire lawn.

Pyrethrum is a natural pesticide made from certain species of the chrysanthemum family that are native to Africa. Its active constituents, pyrethrins and cinerins, are highly effective against aphids, spider mites, and a variety of other leaf-chomping pests. It's also safe and environmentally friendly, since it goes to work quickly, then readily biodegrades in sunlight. In fact, this substance can be applied right up until the time vegetables are harvested and can even be used indoors. Cons: Pyrethrum is toxic to pond fish until it has a chance to biodegrade. Also, pyrethrum-based formulas (it is sometimes combined with neem, another insecticidal and antiseptic plant oil) should not be confused with pyrethroid insecticides. The latter is an entirely different composition and is quite toxic to humans and animals.

ALL-NATURAL PLANT PROTECTION

Many DIY insecticides can be made without making a trip to the garden center. For large gardens, double the recipe and use quart- or gallon-size sprayers. In addition, you may need to reapply these solutions after a heavy rain.

Tea Tree & GSE Fungal Fighter

Diseases such as mildews and fungi can easily be transferred from plant to plant, or even different sections of the same plant, when they hop onto pruning shears as the vehicle. Spray your shears with this simple formula to prevent this disease transfer from happening.

- 2 cups water
- 10 drops grapefruit seed extract
- 10 drops tea tree essential oil

Combine all ingredients into a large spray bottle. Shake well before using on shears. After spraying, wait 2 to 3 minutes before wiping dry with a clean cloth.

All-Natural Aphid Spray

Aphids, also known as plant lice or blackfly, can quickly destroy foliage and spread disease. However, the oils, salts, and acids found in this formula will send them packing just as fast.

1	cup water
1	cup white vinegar
½	cup salt
¼	cup powdered citric acid
¼	cup baking soda
2	teaspoons aloe vera juice
2	teaspoons sesame seed oil
15	drops sage essential oil
10	drops grapefruit seed extract

Combine all ingredients in a large spray bottle. Shake before using, and be sure to apply to the underside of leaves where aphids love to hide.

Get Going Garlic Spray

This formula is effective for most insects, including ants, if sprayed along their routes of travel that bring them to your door.

½	cup flaxseed oil
5–6	garlic cloves, smashed with skins on
2	cups water
1	teaspoon liquid castile soap

Combine the oil and garlic in a bowl. Cover and let sit overnight. Meanwhile, add the remaining ingredients to a large spray bottle. Strain the garlic from the oil, then add the infused oil to the bottle. Shake well before using.

You Say Potato, I Say Tomato

Natural insecticides made from potato starch and tea brewed from leaves of the tomato plant are age–old methods of pest control. This formula brings both together for an extra kick. The result is especially effective against white cabbage butterflies in the vegetable garden.

- 6½ cups water
- 1½ cups fresh tomato leaves, packed
- 2 tablespoons potato flour
- 1 teaspoon liquid castile soap
- 10 drops peppermint essential oil

1. Bring 6 cups of the water to a boil in a medium saucepan. Add the tomato leaves and stir.
2. Remove from the heat, cover, and steep for 30 minutes. Strain off the tomato leaves, reserving the liquid.
3. Add the potato flour to the remaining ½ cup water and blend well (just like you're making gravy). Add the flour mixture to the tomato leaf tea.
4. Add the castile soap and essential oil, stir, and pour into a large spray bottle.

Classic Cayenne Pepper Spray

Since many common garden pests are soft-bodied, they will avoid coming into contact with strong irritants such as onion, garlic, and cayenne pepper. As a bonus, simply omit the soap from this formula, and you've got a great seasoning for a Cajun meal!

- 1 small onion
- 4–5 garlic cloves, skins on
- olive oil
- 1 teaspoon cayenne pepper
- 2 cups water
- 1 teaspoon liquid castile soap

Using a blender or food processor, make a pulp out of the onion and garlic. Spoon the pulp into a small bowl or cup and add just enough oil to cover. Let this mixture rest overnight. In the morning, strain off the oil, then add the cayenne to the oil. Keep this mixture in a glass jar on a shelf for a few days. When ready to use the spray in the garden, combine the water and castile soap in a large bottle. Add 1 teaspoon of the cayenne–olive oil blend, and shake well before applying.

OF MICE & MOLES

Certain plants seem to chase off moles before they can start burrowing into your lawn and uprooting your flowers. These plants include all alliums (such as garlic, onions, leeks, and chives), daffodils, and Mexican marigolds. Castor bean and caper spurge (dubbed "the mole plant") are also effective, but beware: These two plants are poisonous and may not be suitable if small children or pets are present.

Mice don't care for peppermint very much and tend to avoid areas where it grows. Keeping a few potted peppermint plants near the foundation of your home, or giving this mint a place in your culinary herb garden, will help deter them from making their home in yours. If mice seem to be checking out your weekly trash, try adding a few cotton balls moistened with 1 or 2 drops of peppermint essential oil to the top of the garbage heap.

DETERRING DEER

Deer can be a chronic problem for country — and suburban — dwellers. They're very persistent and cunning. The deer's ability to sprint over fences rivals that of an Olympic triathlon gold medalist. They have long memories, too, and always remember where to find a free meal. Fortunately, they can be persuaded to pass up the menu in your garden if you know what they don't like to eat. The big turn-off seems to be any form of decaying animal protein. Smelly? Yes. Effective? Very.

MORE NATURAL DEER GUARDS

Make use of thick shrubbery in your landscaping, such as boxwood, juniper, or holly. Deer won't be so attracted to your yard if they can't see into it, plus a tough thicket is uncomfortable to pass through. Many gardeners report that a few rows of wormwood planted around the perimeter of a property will also discourage deer. When ordering plants from catalogs, look for a deer-resistant rating associated with your selections.

Deer Be Gone

This formula will deter deer from eating your prized shrubbery, ground covers, and other plantings. You can also spray this mixture around the perimeter of your property (the recipe can be doubled, of course) to help keep them from wandering onto your grounds in the first place. Note that a heavy rain will necessitate reapplication. Otherwise, the formula should be reapplied every 2 to 3 weeks.

- 1 cup buttermilk, or regular milk soured with 1 tablespoon white vinegar
- 3 whole eggs, lightly beaten
- 1 teaspoon liquid castile soap
- 1 teaspoon olive oil
- 1 tablespoon Tabasco sauce
- 25 drops clove essential oil
- 1 gallon water, 2 cups removed

Blend all ingredients except the water in a blender or food processor. Using a funnel, pour the mixture into the water in a gallon container. Cap the container and shake well. With a sprayer, apply the mixture to the tops of the plants or the ground you wish to protect. The surface should be lightly sprayed, not saturated.

KEEP PETS OUT OF FLOWER BEDS

If Fido is unearthing your prized tulips, or if Fluffy thinks your rose garden is her outdoor litter box, then you need this simple solution. You can double the recipe if you have a large garden or more than one flower bed.

Out Spot Formula

The scent of this mixture is usually enough to turn your pet away from your plantings. However, you may need to reapply this mixture after a heavy rain or watering.

- ½ cup all-purpose flour
- 3 tablespoons dry mustard
- 1 tablespoon cayenne pepper

Combine all ingredients in a bowl or paper bag. Sprinkle this mixture liberally on the borders of your flower beds, reapplying as necessary.

THE HOME OFFICE

MILLIONS OF PEOPLE IN NORTH AMERICA WORK FROM HOME on a daily basis, and many telecommute at least part-time. Many homes are now equipped with fully functional home offices, where the same germs and grime appear as in traditional office settings.

The formulas and suggestions found in this chapter address equipment common to both. They can also extend to other environments we find ourselves stationed in for significant periods of time, such as hotels, schools, day-care facilities, and college dormitories. To that end, consider this chapter a keep-it-clean-and-green guide when home is where you work, or when you are temporarily away from home.

Why Clean Computer Equipment?

Keeping your home office computer and related equipment clean not only reduces the spread of germs in this often-shared space (what family with kids has a home office that isn't used to do homework, download music, and play video games?) but also extends the life of electronic components. In fact, computer lock-ups and erratic mouse movements can be prevented by routine maintenance. Dust, environmental pollutants, and pet hair can build up inside these items and clog the works. The technical term for this event is known as entropy, and it occurs when household dust naturally gravitates to heat sinks and casings, which serve to pull heat away from sensitive circuitry. If these parts become excessively dirty, a malfunction is sure to follow.

CLEANING ELECTRONIC DEVICES

For better or worse, most of us typically have one or more devices within easy reach. Message notifications, headlines, and reminders all call for our attention throughout the day. Not surprisingly, the exteriors of smart phones and other devices can get pretty grimy and germy, especially if they're shared with other members of your household. All you need to keep your screens clean is a dry, lint-free cloth and one of the gentle cleansers below. A few cotton swabs and a can of compressed air make short work of removing crumbs and dust particles wedged between keys. Note: Be sure to turn off or unplug the device first.

Basic Office Dust- & Germ-Buster

Use this formula to clean the outer surfaces of your office equipment, such as the computer keyboard and monitor (but avoid the glass), printer, and scanner.

- **2** cups water
- **1** cup white vinegar
- **1** teaspoon grapefruit seed extract
- **10** drops sweet orange essential oil

Combine all ingredients in a spray bottle and shake well. Spray directly onto a dry cloth and wipe surfaces clean.

Easy Breezy Glass Cleaner

Monitor screens and the glass surfaces of scanner and copier machines can take on a lot of fingerprints and smudges, or what I call "schmutz." Keep this simple cleaner nearby to keep these surfaces schmutz-free.

> 1 **cup water**
> 1 **cup white vinegar**
> 10 **drops lemon or lime essential oil**

Combine all ingredients in a small spray bottle and shake a few times to blend. Spray lightly onto a cleaning cloth and wipe surfaces until dry. Shake before each use.

WHEN CLEANING ELECTRONICS

Use cotton to clean surfaces since it doesn't produce static electricity like other materials.

Spray the cleaning solutions on the cleaning cloth, not on the component.

Compressed air (or gas) is relatively benign, but make sure the can is recyclable.

· *It's okay to clean the outer workings* of mouse wheels or even disk drives with rubbing alcohol and a cotton swab, but stay away from circuitry.

All-Purpose Cleaning Wipes

With these easy-to-make wipes on hand, keeping your home office fresh and free of germs is just a pop-up away. The basil essential oil is not only antiseptic, it's also stimulating and may increase productivity. You can reuse the cloths after cleaning them in the normal cycle of the dishwasher.

cotton or microfiber cloth

1 cup water

1 cup vinegar

15 drops basil essential oil

Cut the cloth into small squares or rectangles and stack them on top of each other (10 is a good number). Pour the water, vinegar, and essential oil into a heavy-duty ziplock bag. Close the bag and gently squeeze to blend the ingredients. Place your stacked cloth pieces into the bag and close the bag again, pressing down to squeeze out excess air. Use these wipes for quick cleanups, making sure to squeeze out the excess liquid from each wipe first. (*Note:* These are not recommended for nonsealed wood.)

KEYBOARDS

If you tend to snack while you work, there are probably a lot of crumbs lodged in between the keys of your keyboard, which can cause the keys to stop working. Even if you don't eat over the keyboard, it's remarkable how filthy the keys can become over time simply from the oils from your fingers. The remedy for both is to clean the top of each key with a soft cloth moistened with rubbing alcohol or tea tree essential oil and use a cotton swab to get in between keys, if necessary. Either substance will safely and effectively remove built-up grime and kill germs.

If you spill a liquid onto a keyboard, immediately shut off the computer. Then unplug the keyboard and turn it upside down over some towels and allow it to dry out for at least 24 hours. Clean off what sticky residue you can on the outer surface, then see if it will work when you plug it in again. If not, you'll be getting a new keyboard.

Perk Up Office Plants

Plants in your working space offer visual appeal as well as serve as living air purifiers. Here are some suggestions on how to keep these — and even artificial flowers and plants — in good shape.

Unusual but true, milk is actually a great substance to clean dust from plant leaves and give them a beautiful shine. Dip a soft, clean cloth into ½ cup whole or 2 percent milk (use more or less depending on how many plants you have). Squeeze out the excess liquid, then wipe plant leaves clean. Be careful not to let any of the milk pool on the leaves or you'll end up with spots. *Note:* A sock worn over the hand in place of a cloth is perfect for this task.

Cleaning silk or fabric floral arrangements can be tricky since the assembly and components may not hold up to liquid cleaning solutions. If a simple vacuum cleaning is out of the question, try this dry cleaning method to remove the dust and dirt. Pour ½ cup cornmeal and ¼ cup salt into a large paper bag. Place the floral piece into the bag and roll down the top of the bag to form a seal. Shake the bag gently several times. Remove the piece from the bag and carefully brush away any lingering grains of cornmeal or salt.

Spritz away Burnout Fritz

Whether you spend all day in a home office, classroom, or other location, the air can become stale by midday, leaving you feeling sluggish. Closed windows and dry heat in cold climates, or climate-controlled environments in office buildings and hotels, do little to help circulate air. Instead, the only things that may be circulating in these surroundings are germs! Steel yourself against airborne bacteria and brighten your mood and energy level at the same time with these simple herbal aromatics.

No-Flame Gel Candles

These candles lend their scent without having to light them, making them perfect to travel with or to use at home without worrying about small children or pets coming into contact with an open flame. If you keep a lid on the gel candle when it's not in use, the scent should last for several weeks.

- 1 cup cool water
- 1 package powdered gelatin
- ⅛ teaspoon vodka
- ½ teaspoon essential oil of choice

Bring ½ cup of the water to a boil in a saucepan. Add the gelatin to the boiling water, stirring to dissolve. Add the remaining ½ cup water and stir again. Add the vodka and essential oil, and stir until well blended. Pour into a clean glass jar and allow the gel candle to set for about 30 minutes. To use, place the gel candle on a shelf, table, or windowsill, but avoid placing it in direct sunlight or near heat. Keep a lid on the candle when not in use to extend its shelf life.

Warm & Cozy Room Spritzer

This is perfect for those cold winter days when you could use a little extra warmth. As an added benefit, the spritzer's allspice is antiseptic, antibacterial, antifungal, and antiviral.

  1 **cup water**
15 **drops allspice essential oil**
10 **drops cinnamon leaf essential oil**

Combine all ingredients in a small spray bottle. Shake well before using and spritz 2 or 3 times from the center of the room outward in all directions.

TELEPHONE DIRTY TALK TAMER

If you share your home office with other family members, you may be sharing germs when you reach for the phone as well. For that matter, how often do you see your teenager's hands free of his or her smart phone? This simple formula will stop bacteria in its tracks on these devices. Mix 2 tablespoons water with 2 drops of rosemary essential oil and 2 drops of tea tree essential oil. Blend all ingredients in a small bowl or cup. Moisten a soft cloth with this solution and clean the telephone receiver or smart phone screen. Use a second cloth or towel to dry it off.

Clear-the-Air Room Spritzer

This combination provides a fresh, clean scent that won't overpower your senses.

1 cup water
15 drops thyme essential oil
10 drops sage essential oil

Combine all ingredients in a small spray bottle. Shake a few times before using and spray in each direction from the center of the room.

ON THE ROAD, CLEAN AND GREEN

* Take along some All-Purpose Cleaning Wipes (page 208) when you're on the road. They're perfect to use in the car, at school or work, or when you're staying at a hotel.
* Use herbal spritzers to sanitize stuffy air in conference rooms or classrooms, or to freshen hotel linens.
* Bring gel candles with you to improve the scent and the ambience. They travel well, provided they are kept away from direct heat.

INDEX

Page numbers in **bold** indicate tables.

Find More Natural Living Advice with These Books from Storey

Naturally Bug-Free by Stephanie L. Tourles

Protect yourself from mosquitoes, ticks, and other biting insects without relying on chemicals. These 75 all-natural recipes for sprays, balms, body oils, and tinctures — plus herbal pet shampoos, flea collars, and powders — are safe for your body, pets, and home.

The One-Minute Cleaner Plain & Simple by Donna Smallin

Make quick work of housework and use spare moments to dust, swab, polish, and organize. This handbook for busy people has 500 quick tips and strategies for cleaning your home with ease.

Stephanie Tourles's Essential Oils: A Beginner's Guide by Stephanie L. Tourles

Boost your mood, relax your senses, and invigorate your mind with these 100 simple recipes. This friendly guide introduces you to the 25 most versatile essential oils, teaching you how to use these concentrated plant extracts safely and effectively.